For
Randi and
Barclay! Best
wishes !!!
Kyle Miller

Clos de Paris

Dear Randi and Barclay,

So happy to be visiting with you and the turns in Denver. Enjoy the journey my friend takes you on, after deciding to buy a 300 year old farm house in France.

Much love,
Peggy
Feb. 2018

Clos de Paris

Tales of Restoring a Normandy Farmhouse

Kyle Campbell Miller

www.ClosdeParis.com

Written by Kyle Campbell Miller

Edited by Jim Huth

Photographs by Sylvain Bocquet, Kyle and Steve Miller,
Lesley Marciniak, Cyril Besse, Richard Fulton, Peter Adams, and Beverly Teche

Cover art (watercolor painting) by Roger Planson

Clos de Paris: Tales of Restoring a Normandy Farmhouse
ISBN: 978-0-692-63304-5

Published in the United States of America by
MicroPress Books

Printed in the United States of America
First Edition

In memory of our friend and neighbor,

Neville "British Peter" Mullany

DEDICATED TO MY LOVING HUSBAND

AND PARTNER, STEVE

Contents

Part 2 – Renovations and Home Furnishings   47

Part 3 – The Move!   83

Prologue

I've always pictured myself enjoying the *joie de vivre* of France during my advancing years. Perhaps because I'd lived in Europe as a child, or that the French are perpetually planning their next meal — a habit embraced by most senior citizens. Whatever the reason for such a fantasy, I decided to mention the notion to two of my good friends. Agreeing that it really wasn't such a bizarre idea, we began to hunt for a place our families could share in La Belle France. Then, voilà, we found it in the quaint Normandy village of Fresnay-sur-Sarthe.

What followed were six fabulous years of back and forth trips to the "French House," often accompanied by family and friends. But on the final day of our August 2012 visit, my husband, Steve, and I decided to look at a home for sale just down the street from our shared French House. We'd passed the property each time we'd walked up to the village center, and peered through its majestic green gates set in the walls enclosing the property. We were extremely curious to see what lay on the other side.

As we strode in for our scheduled appointment, accompanied by our dear friend, Annie, we were delighted to finally view what had been hidden from sight. The property included more than two acres on the River Sarthe, with sweeping vistas down an expansive hillside to the waterfront. A wide gravel driveway, bordered by a fruit orchard and lined with ancient outbuildings, led to a house and terrace situated high above the river.

The owners were a retired doctor and his wife. The doctor ambled out to greet us, proclaiming as he ushered us inside, *C'est une belle maison!* Madame then met us in the expansive foyer, inlaid with encaustic floor tiles in a mosaic pattern of creams and browns. Our eyes were drawn toward a winding staircase with a curved walnut banister, but before we could discover where it led, we were directed into the parlor.

There we saw another pattern of encaustic floor tiles, as well as a lovely marble fireplace. Deep plaster crown moulding adorned the top of ten-foot walls. And the walls were surprisingly decorated with two nude, impressionist paintings of Madame. The ground floor of the 160-year-old *grande maison* also included a dining room and kitchen. After viewing those rooms, we followed the old couple upstairs to see two additional floors of bedrooms, baths, and unbelievable views. After looking around, we descended a set of backstairs, which connected the larger home to the 300-year-old *petite maison*.

Partitioned into a waiting room, consultation area, and examining room for the doctor's medical practice, the *petite maison* could be accessed from the main house through a door leading from a street-front foyer, as well as through exterior side doors. These latter doorways led to a pathway and garden gate, which were traversed in the past by patients coming to pay the doctor a visit.

Invited to join the owners in the dining room for glasses of Orangina, we admired the fantastic views out of the tall windows. Madame knowingly said with expert salesmanship, *C'est magique.* To further entice us, the couple asked us to linger and inspect the various outbuildings. These structures were charmingly covered in blooming wisteria and climbing roses, and in the past had housed horses, pigs, and chickens.

When we could finally tear ourselves away from the fruit laden trees, flower gardens, and other resplendent scenery, we spied Madame watching from an open window. She leaned out and shouted, *"À bientôt"* — pretty certain that she'd see us again. Steve and I waved goodbye, and then looked at each other and rolled our eyes. However, with Annie's encouragement, we began discussing the possibility of purchasing the French Farmhouse — before we'd even reached the doorway of our shared home, a mere two blocks down the road.

When we learned it was for sale, we took this photo of the house on Clos de Paris.

Back in Florida, Steve and I couldn't dispel the thoughts of the lovely property we'd visited, along with the idea of owning a place all our own in France. We weren't novices at buying and selling real estate. We knew there was lots of homework to be done if this idea was to be seriously pursued. We decided to engage a contractor, whom Annie knew, to inspect the property and interpret the reports supplied to us by the *notaire*.

Miraculously, all reports were declared sound. And, our proposed renovation layout (to convert the doctor's old offices into a large kitchen and family room, and the current dining room and kitchen into a master suite) was pronounced to be straightforward. A general construction budget was drawn up. Doubling the budget to cover unforeseen events and holding our breath, Steve and I made an offer on the house. We envisioned spending long summer months there during our approaching retirement.

Two weeks later the offer was rejected by email. Another two weeks passed, and word came from the *notaire* that there was another bid on the table. We were invited to try again. Increasing the latest offer by a small amount, we received no word for several more weeks and gave up hope. Then a message finally arrived. Our offer was accepted — we'd bought our own home in France!

This book is a collection of emails and pictures sent home during the purchase, renovation, and move into our French Farmhouse. We're confident that you'll delight in meeting our new village friends, and all the hardworking people who made this project possible. And, we hope you'll share in our triumphs as well as our setbacks — while gaining a sense along the way of what we experienced, thanks to the house at Clos de Paris.

A gathering of village friends and neighbors at the home of photographer Sylvain Bocquet (center) in Fresnay-sur-Sarthe. Kyle and her husband, Steve, are third and fourth from the left.

Part 1
Ownership and Demolition

✦

March – April 2013

We've arrived!

The dependable, and noisy, Fresnay greeting party.

Dear Leigh Anne and Reid,

We're back in Fresnay at our jointly owned house! Our first day in France had us devouring fresh eggs supplied to us by our wonderful housekeeper, Lesley. She's agreed to be the caretaker at the new house, too. Hooray! We listened as our neighbor, British Peter, gave us a shout-out on his delightful, weekly radio show. Our walk to the village found open gates and no car at the French Farmhouse, so we poked around and peeked in the windows. It's more spectacular than we remembered — we've made the right decision! After visiting with many of our French friends over lunch in the village, we couldn't resist peering down from the overlook in town at our house-to-be. The doctor and his wife were still moving 35 years' worth of possessions out of their rue du Clos de Paris home.

The closing is set for Tuesday. We bought champagne to pop on the terrace when the house is truly ours. The demolition commences Wednesday in the *petite maison*, so we're enjoying the lull before inevitable issues arise!

Love, Mom and Dad

Ça commence

Dear Kids,

Renovations are set to begin at the Clos de Paris house. Today we had lunch with our cohorts in crime, Annie and Tim. Annie, as you may recall, was the mastermind who put together the French House we now own with our friends. She also sent us our contractor, whom we're to meet tomorrow at a sawmill about an hour from here, to procure "the beam."

With all the discussion which has ensued on how the beam will be delivered, offloaded, and craned over the garden wall, we're thinking of selling tickets in the village for delivery day. Once unloaded, the 25-foot beam is to be hoisted in the air by machine, and sent through a hole in the wall and across the ceiling of the *petite maison* to replace the bearing wall. Then, the temporary supports come out

Annie, our renovation cheerleader.

and... stay tuned. Luckily, your dad, the engineer, is on the job as well.

Tomorrow we have a walk-through with the Doctor and Madame, the current owners, to learn how the windows, gates, fireplaces, etc. all work — then off to the closing with the *notaire* to finalize the purchase. Demolition of the walls in the doctor's former offices to make way for a new kitchen and family room will begin the next day. Later in the week, we're to visit one of Annie's friends whose historic home has a newly installed IKEA kitchen, to see how it all turned out. I think our dance card is full!

I've been supplied with a pile of French decor magazines by Annie, which I'm thumbing through by the fire while sipping white wine. Your dad is in the kitchen, concocting what promises to be a delicious dinner, all while the sun sets over the village. Life is good.

Love, Mom

The French Farmhouse is ours!

Dear Reid and Leigh Anne,

A two-hour walk-through with the former owners, and then a two-hour closing! The house on rue du Clos de Paris is now ours, and even lovelier than we remembered! The doctor and his wife have been careful custodians of the old place.

Lots of stories to tell, but I'm much too pooped to recite tonight. Will write more, between the knocking down of some walls.

Love, Mom

a fire, and a demolition

Dear Kids,

Our purchase of the doctor's home is no longer the talk of Fresnay. Dad and I were locking the gates of our French Farmhouse this evening — after a celebratory toast on the terrace at sunset for surviving the first day of demolition — and we saw flames leaping from a building just down the street in the village. The roof of the building on the corner opposite the pharmacy was on fire. (It also happens to be the office of an insurance agency, where the plate glass window was run through by a motorist speeding down the hill last summer.) We watched as a fireman, perched high above us on a hook and ladder, attempted to douse the flames with a firehose. It took a while, but they succeeded. The road into town was totally blocked with emergency vehicles and sirens. Quite a sight in a small village, and I was thankful that our fire insurance on our new home was up-to-date!

If you can believe it, our first day of knocking out walls was fabulous. We found lovely old beams hidden under the acoustic ceiling in the doctor's former examining room. Best of all, we were able to flip our kitchen plans around so that taking out the bearing wall, which required the delivery of the giant beam, is no longer necessary. (Hooray — worrying about this was keeping me up at night!) The open rooms are more spacious than we thought they'd be, always a plus, as we weren't certain of the thickness of the added partition walls, which we're demolishing. The workmen have been incredibly flexible with the change in plans.

Love and miss you. Until later, Mom and Dad

Keys, and GPS shopping

Things are still proceeding better than expected, but I have a story to tell, which eventually gets back to our renovation work.

Dearest Kids,

Unbeknownst to us, the former owners were instructed by the *notaire* handling the sale of the property to supply us with three sets of keys for the exterior doors. Madame only had two sets. (There are about forty additional keys in a box in the house with handwritten labels in French, which will take a lifetime to decipher.) As we walked together to the lawyer's offices for the closing on Tuesday (what a week) Madame veered off to the magazine/newspaper store to retrieve the last

Cyril opens a long-closed doorway, which connects the parlor to the future kitchen.

required set of keys she'd ordered to be made. As it turns out, they don't make them on-site at this particular shop (as they do at the hardware store a block away) and they weren't there to be picked up. Madame then instructed us to pick them up after the closing. We obligingly stopped by to do so, but were told they still weren't on-site from wherever they send them to be made.

The next day we returned once again to attempt to retrieve our new set of keys from the paper shop. It seems that a local plumber had stopped by before we'd arrived. While chatting with the shopkeeper, he'd mentioned that he was doing some work at our shared French House. So that's when she decided to give OUR set of keys to the plumber to give to us. We decided that this would only happen in a very small French village.

The afternoon was spent shopping for armoires, as well as looking for kitchen tiles and terrace stones with Annie and Tim. With no time to stop at every

shop, they'd blink their car headlights as we passed by one of their favorite places on the way to another. We'd then dutifully enter the locale into our GPS to return to it some other day. Back in Fresnay, we stopped in to see the latest progress at chez number two. The correct items had been ripped out by our worker, Cyril, and all is starting to take shape. Tomorrow is another day, and hopefully there will be time for laundry.

We hope all is going great with each of you, Campbell, and Margo. Things here are proceeding incredibly well. It was a leap of faith to do this, and seems to have been a good gamble. You will all love this gorgeous place!

Love and miss you, Mom

The all-powerful mayor of Fresnay

Dear Lovely, Grown Children,

We have clean clothes again! We also spoke to three serious looking, but very professional, chaps yesterday regarding the roof of *petite maison*. Prior to making our offer on the house, we discovered that the ancient clay tiles on this area of the roof had to come off, the underneath re-felted, and the old tiles returned to what would be a newly insulated house top. We've since found that one of the chimneys also needs work, as we'll be utilizing it with the added fireplace in the family room. (An old hearth was discovered in this room behind the peeling plaster.) All of this outside work has to be done authentically because we are on the "list."

It seems that our "new" house is a registered historic landmark — although in a small village with the remains of a fort dating back to the 9th Century it's hard to imagine what wouldn't be considered old! As you know, Dad and I owned the historic Beardall Home in Orlando for twenty years, so we're used to asking permission from a committee of citizens before undertaking any architectural changes. But here in Fresnay, the mayor is known as "The Decider."

The chimney inspection included a scenic view of the village below.

Luckily, a few years ago, our dear friend and neighbor, "British Peter," decided to throw a soirée to introduce us to the important people in Fresnay. Steve and I received the guest list in advance, and we practiced pronouncing names, as well as a question to pose to each person in French. This worked out well, as when we asked our question, our new acquaintance would respond for several minutes while we nodded and said, "Oui;" although, most of the time, we had no idea what they were saying. (Even now, when we meet a former party guest on the street they begin to speak to us — seemingly where we left off — and we continue to nod and agree.) As you may have guessed by now, the mayor was one of Peter's invitees.

The village castle, with an office for "The Decider" on the right.

Dad and the mayor conducted a lively, albeit mostly one-sided conversation at the party. As you well know, your Dad is not shy. He's been known to speak English with a French accent, as well as to resort to pantomime. This seems to work for him, and in the course of their repartee at Peter's party, Dad learned that the mayor is very fond of American bourbon. It was then that he decided to bring back a bottle of Knob Creek bourbon from Duty Free on our next visit to Fresnay. He did, and presented it to the mayor. He in turn wrote us a lovely thank you note, acknowledging how much he appreciated the gift. We're hoping that propositions put to His Honor regarding our new house will be as favorably received!

Love, Mom

A gardener hired,
a fireplace designed,
and armoires purchased

Dear Leigh Annie and Reid, here's another update. Miss you all!

Today we spent considerable time walking around our newly acquired property with a professional gardener, Monsieur Roulin, who speaks no English whatsoever. Luckily for us (this phrase seems to come up quite often lately) his son, Oliver, handles the communications between his English-speaking clients and his father. This is usually done over the phone with the receiver handed back and forth. I've yet to meet Oliver, but feel that he is likely to become our new best friend.

As you've seen from the pictures, our recently purchased gardens are quite expansive, and we learned a lot more about them on our stroll today with Monsieur Roulin — via phone translations with Oliver. It seems we have three cherry trees, two fig trees, several apple trees, two pear trees, and various other blooming plants, hedges, and garden plots, which Monsieur Roulin assures us will be *très belle* once he trims, weeds, and shapes. While we're fortunate enough to have acquired this new property mortgage free, we may yet be required to assume one in order to afford Monsieur Roulin.

On a cost savings note, we had some luck designing our new fireplace. Stored in the barn are various old tiles and bricks. One stack of bricks are stamped or molded with a somewhat floral and vine design. It turns out that there are enough of these old bricks to make lovely mantel supports, as well as a hearth. We then began to cast about for ideas for the mantel, and remembered an old beam we'd found on the property. It's the perfect size, and so voilà, the materials are on hand for our mason, Cyril, to assemble a lovely new fireplace.

This all happened before lunch, so after a quick bite at the Alps Mancelle Restaurant in our village, we shot off to a *brocante* in Alençon to purchase the three armoires we'd seen with Annie and Tim two days prior. There are no closets in these old houses, so they are a necessity. Looking them over once again, we made our decision and began to haggle with the very nice shop keeper. We ended up with all three beautiful clothes cupboards at a deep discount plus free delivery — a truly successful shopping expedition!

A Renault dealership was conveniently located next door to the aforementioned *brocante*. As we peered through the fence, a man was locking up, and had what appeared from a distance to be a large pierced earring (it turned out to be a phone earpiece). He told us to please come in and have a look. We did, and we found the perfect used car — an automatic diesel, with low mileage at a decent price. Unlike the *brocante* next door, however, the price was not negotiable. Apparently, in France, used cars are the one thing you don't haggle over. We asked for his card to think about it, and discovered he was the proprietor. Deciding that we'd made enough decisions for one day we left through the gate — and watched as the owner wheeled out of the car lot... on his bicycle.

Love, Mom

We survived seven hours at IKEA!

We're in the midst of electrical and plumbing decisions, as well as fireplace design. Still having fun, but working very hard. We even had to navigate between various French egos yesterday morning. Today we make a two-hour trip to IKEA in Caen. Going to a big box store to me is like a venture into hell — but they have nice wood cabinets and Whirlpool appliances, so wish us luck, and English-speaking assistance!

Dear Sweet, Big Kids,

Taking apart this old house to uncover its true bones and hidden surprises has been a delight. Behind the demolished walls and other false partitions in the old doctor's offices are pantries we hadn't realized existed, as well as window alcoves with rough cut and irregular stone sills. Ancient clay floor tiles peek up at you around the edges of the peeled back linoleum. Plaster walls hide behind the glue when the contact paper is removed, and hand hewn beams are exposed beneath acoustic ceiling tiles. Given these delightful and unique characteristics, we want to create a modern kitchen in keeping with the old farmhouse cottage we've discovered in the 18th century *petite maison*.

After a seven-hour quest in IKEA (about an hour-and-a-half ride to the north of us in Caen) we emerged barely functioning but still smiling — thanks to magnificent help from IKEA employee, Cedrick — who put together a computerized, order ready, product list, along with a three-dimensional drawing of our new kitchen. As you know, I'd done as much homework ahead of time as I could in the U.S., selecting cabinets, listing product codes, and laying out a kitchen that would fit in our proposed spaces. Transposing American sizes from inches into centimeters also gave us a head start. Of course, the cabinet dimensions are somewhat different in France, and the model numbers are not the same — even for the same products — but it gave us a blueprint with which to begin.

There are some products in the French IKEA store that we didn't find in the US. In Caen we fell in love with a cabinet made out of silver birch, slightly washed in off-white so that the pinkish wood grain is evident, a nice companion to what will be our rehabilitated and polished clay tile floors. The fronts are embellished with double beveled panels very similar to the paneled doors throughout the house. We selected thick natural wood countertops with a slightly reddish cast, rather than yellow, to keep the palette coordinated.

Our plans include one wall to house the oven/microwave, counter space, glass wall cabinets, stove top, and refrigerator. The generous island will employ a sink, dishwasher, garbage can, additional drawers, a small wine rack, and shelves for cookbooks. The appliances are stainless steel — sorry 18th century! We're keeping the Doctor's white double porcelain sink at the end of the kitchen as an extra pair of *les lavabos*. The hard part now will be to lay out the electrical and plumbing, and then to hear how much more must be torn apart to accomplish the plan. Two steps forward — one step backward.

We may be back to the drawing board on the fireplace design as well, as we got an "Mmmmmm" out of Annie when she saw it. Experienced in creating authentically renovated homes in this part of France, she let us know that stone, not brick, is the material used in traditional Normandy fireplaces. Now that the kitchen is resolved, we'll go looking for stones. But tomorrow, it is the cable company in Le Mans (and my nail appointment — some things still take priority) to set up Wi-Fi and cable locations at the house before the plaster walls are repaired. We've definitely made a lot of progress in the seven days since our closing, and so we took Sunday off to attend the circus (another story) and to lunch with friends.

Love and miss you, Mom

A sandblaster, the circus, a celebratory dinner, and Easter eggs on the doorstep

Today I need to organize receipts from Cyril, as well as our newly established house accounts, and of course catch up on laundry. But first, I wanted to write you about what's been happening since my last update.

Dear Kids,

You haven't lived until you've listened to four Frenchmen discuss how much they're going to charge you, the bystanders, to rent a sandblaster for 24 hours. As I related to you previously, we uncovered lovely beams in what will be our new kitchen. Unfortunately, they've been painted red — hence the need for this equipment to remove the paint and restore them to their natural state.

Not only was the rental price exorbitant, now they wanted a check for twice the rental sum — not a credit card — as a deposit. Since they're also delivering and picking up the machine, I thought that rather unnecessary, as we aren't planning on leaving the area to sandblast our way across France in our spare time. But I wrote out the check, and as with the rest of this venture, took a leap of faith that they wouldn't cash it and run off to the south of France for warmer weather — it's freezing here.

As I'm writing this update, your dad is out riding along on the "new" riding lawn mower. It had been duly demonstrated to us by the doctor before purchase to seal the deal. (I rescued his cane, which he nearly backed over in the process.) As you know, Dad loves machinery, and yesterday he drove the tractor up onto rails to clean out the five pounds of dried grass which had accumulated underneath it, as well as to sharpen the blades. I have visions of amputated feet and hands, or of him rolling down the slope with the tractor tumbling on top of him. Instead of wringing my hands and watching, I'm staying out of sight. Also, since Cyril and his helper, Will, are sandblasting away inside, there's no place for me on-site today anyway.

This is getting lengthy, and I still have to set up online house accounts — which I dread — so I'll wind up by telling you that the Fresnay-sur-Sarthe Circus School is a delight. A recent New York Times article reported that the French Department of Culture is supportive of French circus education (which seems a bit strange) and therefore forty circus schools have sprung up throughout France. We have one in Fresnay, complete with a permanent big top tent near the old railway station. We treated Annie and Tim, along with their British contractor friend, John, to a show on Sunday.

John has been renovating homes in France for 25 years, and he'd independently looked over the French Farmhouse buildings before our purchase to assure us that the wiring, etc., hadn't been done by someone's brother-in-law. A day at the circus seemed a fine way to treat all three of them for their generous help. Anyway, at the show two very muscular young men tumbled, juggled, and stood on their hands before us. It made me want to go home and do stretches. The audience, including many French children, was as much fun to watch as the show.

Last but not least, Canadian Peter and Lynda, who previously owned a share in the French House but have also since bought their own home in Fresnay, were kind enough to invite us over for dinner last night. Champagne was uncorked to celebrate our crazy adventure. It was very thoughtful, as we've been too tired to cook for ourselves. Over dinner, they told us that the latest questions in the village about the Clos de Paris home were either, "How many families are moving into this house?" or, "Is it going to be a hotel?" It was a delightful evening, and when we came home we found that British Peter had left us three hand-painted Easter eggs on our doorstep.

Love, Mom

A Word about Cyril, and other odds and ends

I hope you're headed into a lovely Easter weekend. It has been relentlessly freezing cold here, but we're proceeding ahead undaunted. Here's the latest.

Dear Sweet Kids,

I've mentioned our wonderful worker, Cyril, but now I'd like to tell you a bit more about him. In picturing Cyril, think of a slight, but very strong, young Frenchman with dark hair, who is always smiling (except when photographed) and ever polite. When he stops his frenetic pace of work to discuss an issue that needs resolving, the makings of tiny hand-rolled cigarettes are ever present. It's mesmerizing to watch him take an infinitesimal piece of brown cigarette paper, drop in loose tobacco, and expertly wrap it up all together — while never losing eye contact with you.

If he doesn't light up immediately, he will dangle the handmade cigarette behind his ear, where it sways and loses bits of tobacco as he gestures and converses with us in a mixture of English and French. He blessedly knows enough English for us to communicate, although if we reach an impasse in our mutual comprehension his fall-back phase is always, "As you wish!" It's as if we have our very own genie who would grant our heart's desire — if he could only understand what it was.

I have to say there is nothing that Cyril cannot or will not tackle. No matter what issue arises, he assures us that he can resolve it — and he does. Knowing that the cost per 24 hours of equipment rental is

Cyril in the midst of kitchen renovation work.

high, he and his very able assistant, Wilfred, will work until 8:00 p.m. — then begin again early the next morning so it can be returned within a day. Whatever ideas we discuss, Cyril usually has a suggestion — where to put an outlet or outside faucet, or how to better show off a delightful architectural detail — that makes it all just a little bit better. And if we say something he doesn't quite understand, Wilfred, normally silent, will translate for us all and then smile. They are two of the hardest working men of any nationality I've ever met, and they certainly put the rumor to rest that their countrymen are a bunch of slackers.

And our gardener, Monsieur Roulin, who is in his seventies, is certainly no slouch himself! He arrived today with a three-story extension ladder and shimmied way up into a conifer tree with a gas powered chainsaw. He corralled your dad into holding onto a rope tied to various tree branches so he could yank them

Monsieur Roulin and Steve trimming a tree by the woodshed.

as they fell and prevent them from landing on our woodshed roof. Remarkable!

We left everyone toiling away at the house, and we ended the day with another trek to Alençon to look at yet another fireplace mantel, and then made a quick stop by Brico Depot. At this new store, which resembles Home Depot, you drive your car into the product yard, load your car, truck, or available tractor, and drive up to a cash out window. It was there that Dad had to recall *quatre vingt-seize* to cash out with the 96 fire bricks we'd loaded into the trunk of our rental car. It was another full and blessed day in La Belle France.

Joyeaux Pâques! Love, Mom

Snow, Dad's brocante adventure, and Simon says

I had to stop writing last night to enjoy the sunset over our new terrace. Here's the latest.

Dear Kids,

It appeared that Santa was on his way in place of the Easter Bunny when we woke up the day before Easter to see fat snowflakes falling outside our bedroom windows. Dad set off to purchase the decided upon (finally) fireplace mantel at the

Espirit Brocante with cash from both of our ATM cards. Our salesman, Richard (pronounced Reeeechar) with whom we'd negotiated earlier, would only accept cash for the agreed upon price.

Dad arrived at the place of purchase, a huge old farm complex now covered in snow, but neither Richard nor anyone else of assistance could be found. Wandering into the onsite restaurant, Dad found two other customers imbibing in a glass of wine at 11:00 in the morning. Introductions were made all around as well as with Katerine, who was serving the morning alcohol. Dad struck a bargain with the group. If no able-bodied assistance could be found, then he would help them to load their purchases, if they would agree to help him negotiate our mantel — along with the 180-pound fireplace heating plate tossed into the bargain — into our car. The deal was sealed over another glass of wine.

Once our purchases were stowed, it was Dad's turn to help his new friends with what turned out to be a truckload of furniture. Ready to roll, but with still no one to pay, another glass of wine was had by all (Dad claims that the glasses were very small) until Richard finally appeared. Dad proceeded to hand over the entire sum in twenty euro notes supplied via the ATM. Richard immediately hid the cash from public view and counted it behind the bar. Steve wheeled away in the once again fully loaded rental car, but not before teaching Richard and Katerine the American saying, "Cash on the barrelhead!"

Meanwhile, I'm back in Fresnay standing on the corner at the five-way intersection we lovingly refer to as "malfunction junction," peering into every white work van that went by. I was looking for a man named Simon, who'd been recommended by a friend of a friend as the IKEA kitchen installer in Normandy. I was bundled up like a mummy, but even a grandmother swathed in clothing while standing on a corner looking at Frenchmen will get stares and honks in France. It was an uncomfortable ten minutes, which could have all been avoided.

For you see, as I would soon learn, Simon is a very literal man — which is an excellent trait in a kitchen installer, but not so much when you tell him to look for an American in a blue scarf, and then you wear green. Searching for that blue scarf, he passed me several times. Finally, he pulled over and I climbed into the cab of his truck alongside him, his wife Pauline, and their French Poodle, Teddy.

Now that we'd located each other, we headed to what had once been a home, but is now a construction site. Upon arrival, Simon measured and penciled in the kitchen on the newly sandblasted floor. He also looked over the IKEA printout of the proposed itemized purchases. About the time that Simon was adding a few trim pieces before proclaiming the order to be in good shape, your Dad rolled in, feeling no pain from his sojourn at the *brocante*.

Finished with our work in the kitchen, we set off for lunch with Annie and Tim, who had joined us to add their requested advice. Afterward, with cheek kisses all around, Simon assured us that he would install a splendid kitchen at the house. Then he, Pauline, and their poodle drove away. Now we're free to travel once again to IKEA on Tuesday to finalize the purchases, and to take advantage of the spring sale — which might cover the cost of the sandblaster, but who's counting euros at this point?

Love you guys! Mom

Easter Mass, Lesley's chicks, and the Gastronomique

Today was uneventful, thank goodness, with just a walk-through with the electrician. (I made sure everyone had enough outlets in their bedrooms and baths for lamps and hairdryers.) We fed the goats at the top of our hill, and saw the three new black lambs. A rooster wandered onto our new terrace today, which was a surprise. Here is what happened yesterday.

Dear Family,

It's quite an experience, sitting in a centuries-old church listening to Mass being read and sung in the musical French language. The choirmaster was in top

Easter Sunday at the village church in Fresnay-sur-Sarthe.

form on Easter Sunday. (Several years ago, I came in the open side door, was handed music and accidentally became part of the choir — but that's another story.)

The elderly local priest serves fourteen village churches in the area, confirming reports of the shortage of up-and-coming Catholic clergy. There's a schedule on the church door which tells you where Mass will be held on a given Sunday. As Fresnay has one of the more majestic and important churches in the area, Mass is held here on all the important days in the liturgical calendar.

We were due for lunch at Sillé Beach; so, being non-Catholics who cannot partake in the Eucharist, we bolted when the good Catholics rose for Communion. Lesley and John, the caretakers of the French House (as well as our soon-to-be French Farmhouse on rue du Clos de Paris) had invited their "clients" for Easter lunch. There were over forty guests composed of Brits, some Irish and a few scattered French. Almost all are owners of second homes in France, whom Lesley has dubbed as her "Chicks." She and John do in fact watch out for us all in our absence, and so the name is apt. It was evident that they are well-loved by all in attendance, and from the size of the group we feel very fortunate to be a part of their clutch of peeps.

Lunch was entertaining in many respects. I was seated next to one of the few Frenchmen present. Seinfeld would describe him as a "close-talker." I spent the first hour with him conversing with me in French at a distance of about two-inches from my nose. It turns out that he works for a charitable organization, and has traveled to Rwanda and Mali assisting victims of genocide.

On the opposite end of the spectrum, we enjoyed two paid vocalist's. You've never heard "Itsy Bitsy Teenie Weenie Yellow Polkadot Bikini" (we *WERE* at the beach) until you've heard it sung in French by a woman whose jet black hair matched her skin-tight, leather pants. Actually, she and her male companion were quite good. Urged on at one point by Phillip, a fellow guest sporting an eye patch and who is an English Barrister (the one who wears the wig and argues in court) we gave them a standing ovation.

As if we hadn't had enough excitement for one day, the entire party continued on a little further down the road after lunch for the annual Gastronomique in the charming village of St. Leonard des Bois. At this annual event, you may taste and purchase champagne, wine, pâté, pastries, and even escargot. After a few sips and purchases, we loaded up in the car and came back for a quiet evening in Fresnay. The sun cooperated, so we bundled up and stood on the terrace of our construction site and watched the sunset. Walking back, we were invited in for drinks by our neighbor Sara (another one of Lesley's peeps, but that's another story). Easter is pretty neat in Fresnay.

Love, Mom

Sunset from the terrace of our Clos de Paris home, overlooking the Sarthe River.

Marital minefield, torchis, an old newspaper, and "National Park Roulin"

Dear Wonderful Kids,

There were a few terse moments, but Dad and I are still speaking after our second trip to IKEA in a week. Dad calls it the yin and yang of our collaborative efforts — at times I call it something else! Our hearts sank when we were told that Cedrick was on vacation. But, Camille gamely stepped forward and agreed to dive into the order of *Les Américain* after her lunch break. So, off we went to eat at the IKEA cafeteria.

Camille was true to her word, and she went over each and every item, including the meters of toe kick. This is the fourth kitchen that Dad and I have planned together from scratch, and we've learned a lot about what we do and don't want — yinning and yanging along the way. But I must say, ordering and installing one in France has been an added challenge. Anyway, all is now ordered and the VISA card was accepted. Dad is happily perusing an IKEA catalogue for a future spending spree, as we've been granted a large store credit for taking advantage of their spring sale. *Très bien!* We returned to Fresnay to check on our "boys" who'd given up the ghost, but had left behind evidence of their day's work.

Torchis is a special building material used in old structures in Europe. It's made from a mixture of mud, straw, and fine gravel. Oh, and cow dung is added for adhesion. There is ancient *torchis* in our ceilings at the French Farmhouse. One day, Cyril had pried up the floor tiles in the attic, and he'd carefully lifted the mixture out of one spot, to peer down and determine the height of the beams below. (They'd been hidden from view by the acoustic ceiling tiles.) All of the ancient materials had been lovingly saved in a wagon to be replaced, and today was that day.

Yesterday we discovered an old local newspaper, dated December, 13, 1956, behind the porcelain sinks — and still in excellent condition. A picture of Eisenhower graced the front page. One article was reported by a Jean Eskenazi, whose byline claimed he'd just departed Melbourne for France on a Pan American Stratocruiser. He wrote that the Americans had soundly beaten the Aussies in competitive swimming, winning more gold medals during the Olympics than anyone else that year. I've yet to translate the rest of it, though the find was poignant for me, as it was published while I was a child living in Germany during the Cold War. One never knows what discoveries will show up next within the walls of this old house.

The old newspaper we found behind the doctor's porcelain sinks.

But this evening's house visit did reveal Monsieur Roulin toiling away — rapidly creating our own national park. (He was even here the day it snowed!) My favorite French phrases to him are, *Nous ne serions pas ici cette année* and

L'année prochaine. But, he is determined to tame the overgrown flower beds and trees *THIS* year, and to subdue it all *correctement.* His hoeing and trimming have revealed planting areas, stepping stones, and vistas we didn't know existed. Years of neglect by two elderly people who could no longer enjoy their gardening had created botanical chaos. Once under control, Monsieur Roulin assures us that it will be much easier (and cheaper) to maintain the grounds. Like all of the people helping to make this wonderful place into a home, he's a treasure whom we sincerely appreciate.

Love, Mom

More evidence of Monsieur Roulin's magique *in the gardens.*

Armoire delivery, and the local hardware store

We had a successful changing of the guard here — Dad left on one train, and Kathy arrived on another. She came home, downed Dad's chicken soup, and insisted on seeing the French Farmhouse before her shower. She's now sleeping soundly in our jointly owned French House, so I have a chance to recap the latest events.

Dear Kids,

How do you squeeze an eight-foot armoire through a spiral staircase upstairs to a bedroom? We found out — it's not easily done. Dad ran up the backstairs to help direct the action, while the others heaved it up the front staircase. It was quite the scene. The picture attached is more descriptive than any written words. Will, Cyril, and even Yoann, the soon-to-be electrician (pictured in the foreground) jumped into the fray.

But back to the armoires... two were successfully lofted up the staircase, and one is now ensconced in our soon-to-be bedroom on the ground floor. We were impressed with Cyril's leadership during the process. While straining under the load of a large piece of furniture, he shouted orders at all to prevent their running

Our crew carefully maneuvered both armoires up and through the stairwell.

into walls and door jams. We are now well prepared to hang clothes... once we have a kitchen, walls without holes, etc., etc. The afternoon ended with our interview of a painter, and a discussion of the electrical bid with Yoann. We are deliberating on the painting bid, but accepted the electrical Devis. Yoann is no dummy. Hauling armoires for us was an excellent prelude to our business conversation!

It's been cold this week, but we finished the day on the terrace once again at sunset. This time we were joined by British Peter, as well as by Canadian Peter and Lynda. We popped more champagne — it is crazy cheap over here — and toasted to warmer occasions. (We've been very envious of the Jacksonville and Los Altos weather reports.)

Madame proprietor and her well-stocked hardware store.

Locking the gate after our soirée reminded me to tell you about our amazing village hardware store. The large gate key resembles a Disney prop, and copies can't be whipped up on any new-fangled machine, so we took it to the Bricolage Shop to have extras created by hand. We needed several sets to parcel out to our plethora of contractors.

This shop is jam-packed, but the proprietor knows her inventory. There you can find anything and everything you could possibly require, but at a price she often tells you is *très cher*. We once had guests who were kind enough to offer to buy a real set of barbecue tools for the French House. It was October and not outdoor party season in Fresnay, so none were available at the more reasonably priced stores. But our guests were insistent, so we stopped by the hardware store and queried Madame. She took us through three doorways, a closet, and at last to a box on a shelf where, voilà, there was a full set.

Love and miss you, Mom

The old-fashioned gate keys at Clos de Paris.

The tourist office, bees, surprises, and aperitifs

Dear Family,

You never know what you'll spy when you peer in at the window in the tourist office in Fresnay-sur-Sarthe. Due to different departures and arrivals at the train station, we'd missed British Peter's radio show of events that would take place over the weekend and were "not to be missed." So, after gathering food at the wonderful Fresnay Saturday market, Kathy and I strolled over to peruse the event posters that are always on display.

Two of our favorite vendors at Fresnay's Saturday market.

We quickly ruled out a reggae dance to be held in a neighboring village accompanied by a Caribbean style dinner. Other events, such as a play with dual roles played by a male thespian in drag, sounded interesting, but would debut after our departure from France. We then noticed the poster regaling "free admission today" at the nearby Bee Museum. Deciding this would be part of our afternoon plan, we made a last stop at the local cafe to greet the owners, Martine and Pierre, and to share a cup of coffee with British Peter. The latter berated us for daring to miss his radio show, even as he scanned the daily horse racing sheets to select his bets.

After the plat du jour at the Alps Mancelle restaurant and a surprising visit at the French Farmhouse with Cyril (more on this later) Kathy and I set off to search the countryside for the Musee des Abeilles. We drove around the general vicinity, and were certain we'd found the spot when a person, standing at the edge of the road dressed as a giant bee, waved and directed us into a parking lot.

The place was abuzz with activity, and thus began our education on everything bee. First, we encountered a large display of antique *les ruches*, made

My friend, Kathy, at the Musee des Abeilles, which features an unusual collection of beehives from around the world

from reeds and clay, with tops that resembled hats worn by the "tin man" in the Wizard of Oz. Then our tour continued through a collection of ancient tools with bellows, which were used to smoke the insects out of their hives in order to collect their combs.

Next, we were treated to archaic presses which would squeeze the honey from the combs and render the sought after nectar. We ended with a jaunt through the gift shop, where we stocked up on bee shaped soaps for our grandchildren, but rejected the stuffed bee toys, which looked more like strange, striped bears with wings.

And now, I'll tell you more about our earlier visit with Cyril at the house today. Imagine my surprise when a bright light appeared to be emanating from deep within the hall closet, which is located underneath the front staircase. I peered in, and I could surprisingly see the basement below, and Will laboring in it. It seems there had been quite a miscommunication. My item to Cyril of, "Please cover the low ceiling above the stairs to the basement from the kitchen with insulation" (to prevent brain damage) became "please build another set of stairs to the wine cellar." You may be wondering how that is even possible, as did I.

On one of our first visits to the house, we had discussed the idea of a new basement staircase. However, once Cyril had projected the cost, we'd rejected it in favor of spending the money elsewhere. Somehow, Cyril hadn't gotten this message, although it should have given me a clue when he notated "wood or cement" next to this item on his list. Anyway, work on said staircase was halted with apologies all around, and plans were made to replace the back wall of the closet.

Cyril was quite upset about something else as well, as the day before he'd come to say the words I both dreaded and expected... "I have bad news!" It seems that Will's wife, an experienced wallpaper stripper, had come to perform this job at our house. Unfortunately, underneath the awful orange paper in our foyer was yet another layer of wallpaper which had also been painted, so all was not successfully stripping away. Relieved that it wasn't something worse, I said not to worry, we would deal with that another day — please get back to the plumbing and electrical work. Embarrassed by the lack of success as if it was their fault, no one would let me pay the woman for her considerable time and effort that day attempting to remove wallpaper.

The day ended with a visit by the painter to the French House to talk about the stripping and revarnishing of that front door (seems to be a theme in this missive). Having obtained a price from him for this job, he chatted with us over a beer and then departed. On his heels came Monsieur Roulin, who'd been invited over to meet Kathy, as she'll be dealing with him at the French House when we move down the street. We had a lively conversation over aperitifs about the French names for daffodils (*les jonquilles*) and wisteria (*les glycines*). Kathy decided that she needed a broader French gardening vocabulary, and I was just pleased that everyone hit it off so well. We both agreed that these two men took their disparate professions very seriously. It was a good beginning to her stay with me in Fresnay.

Love and miss you all, Kyle/Mom/Kiki

Ancient floor tiles, McDonald's, and a hearthstone

I'm a little behind with your Dad being gone, but here is what happened on Monday.

Dear Family,

It was a daunting task. Cyril informed me that an additional 500 *ancienne* terra cotta floor tiles would be necessary to replace the damaged ones in our soon-to-be kitchen and TV room. In French, these square, unglazed, floor tiles are called *les carreaux*. They were created in various dimensions, thicknesses, and colors. (The hexagon shaped ones are called *tomettes* — which we can happily claim in the upstairs bedrooms.)

A few dozen *les carreaux* had been located in the barn, but that number would not suffice. On an earlier foray, I'd spied crates of these tiles at the Espirit Brocante, where we'd purchased our fireplace mantel. Annie informed me that we might also find them at the Brocante Depot. So, off Kathy and I went, sample tile in hand, to wander the *brocantes* of Normandy in the freezing rain. (Kathy emphasizes that it was "long underwear freezing!")

We arrived at the Espirit Brocante, which as I told you earlier is an old, converted farm complex. During Dad's wine drinking adventure, it was covered in a blanket of snow. This April day was not much warmer. Kathy and I wandered through the former barnyard, which still sports chickens and various pet dogs. (Did I mention it is seriously cold?) Lugging the tile around, I placed it next to others for sale in various crates throughout the compound until we found a match. "Reeechard" was once again nowhere in sight, so following Dad's lead we entered the *brocante* restaurant.

Alas, it was closed for lunch so we were unable to meet the lusty Katerine, but we did find Antony. He accompanied me outside to the correct batch of tiles, and we began to bargain. There were only 370 *les carreaux* in the crate. Thinking of the old adage "a bird in the hand," I struck an agreement with Antony, who promised they'd be delivered that evening. He added that upon delivery, at such a good price, it must naturally be "cash on the barrelhead!"

Deprived of sustenance, Kathy and I drove to the Brocante Depot, owned and operated by the two Chauvin sisters. The sign on the gate informed us that they were off enjoying their own lunch, and the store would reopen in thirty minutes. As you know, in France it is *très difficile* to be served lunch in short order, so we made a very American choice and headed for McDonald's. Fortified with fast food, we drove back to the store to begin our search of the outdoor displays for the remainder of the requested number of floor tiles. We found terra cotta roof shingles, stones, and every other item except *les carreaux*.

Then, voilà, there at the far end of the yard was a match — 1,500 of my identically sized floor tiles in the correct color — a miracle. I dragged Madame out to look, and she sadly shook her head. Yes, they were for sale, but not a mere 170. Only the entire stack could be purchased! Seriously dejected, I pleaded my case. Madame finally relented, and agreed to sell me half the tiles. This would mean 750 tiles at 100 euros less than the 370 *les carreaux* from the first *brocante* — and she accepted VISA! The deal was struck, and I called Antony to cancel. He pretended not to understand either Kathy or me.

Feeling victorious, we returned to Fresnay just in time for me to decide where the hearthstone should lay inside the new fireplace. Tim, Annie, Dad, and I had previously selected a nice granite stone from the garden. This seemed like a fine idea at the time until they all deserted me, and I was left to figure out its final resting place. Cyril, always trying to please, usually gives me several options too many. He always asks me, his mouth clenching the ever present cigarette, "Do you want it like zis, like zis, like zis, or like zis?" Whenever I ask him what *HE* thinks, the answer is always, "As you like!" In utter frustration, we called in Yoann and Will. A unanimous decision was finally made, and a hearthstone was laid in our new Miller homestead.

Love, Kyle/Mom/Kiki

Cyril, hard at work on the new fireplace.

Brocante jaunt, deliveries, and Monsieur Roulin's bill

Here is a catch-up missive. Kathy and I enjoyed pizza by the fireplace in the Bourgneuf House at day's end.

Dear Family,

It was a great plan. We were to meet Annie and Tim in a *brocante* parking lot in the little Normandy town of Ferté Macé, and proceed from there to lunch. Then we were to head onward to Antiquités du Donjon (which actually does translate as "Antiques Dungeon") in the fortified old city of Domfront, north of Fresnay-sur-Sarthe. Kathy and I plugged the first town into our GPS, and off we went.

Steve and I call our Garmin GPS the French Lady, although the instructive voice has a distinctly British accent. She also has a mind of her own. Unless you're careful, she'll send you to your destination via farm roads and middle-of-nowhere places. Of course, Kathy and I would rather chat, so we submissively followed her advice, and drove toward our rendezvous on roads less traveled.

Yet, we were punctual when we greeted our friends, although the *brocante* in front of us was closed. (It was Tuesday and not lunchtime, so go figure.) We gathered into one car and set off for the next destination. Suffice to say we had a wonderful three course lunch (not quick) and found some treasures, for which we bargained and arranged deliveries. We returned to our car, which was parked in front of the not-to-be-patronized *brocante*, and drove back to Fresnay (via the highways) just in time for me to make further decisions on the fireplace — agh!

On Wednesday I met two delivery trucks — one with a lovely cabinet purchased at the Antiquités du Donjon in Domfront the day before. The delivery truck was towing a trailer loaded with an ancient glass and wooden ticket booth, such as you'd see at an old carnival. Hoping they hadn't confused my purchase, I was relieved when they opened the van and my treasure emerged. As the *brocante* owner surveyed the size of the empty house, he winked at me and said upon leaving, "*À bientôt*." He was pretty certain he'd see me again.

The next delivery was 768 *les carreaux* (according to Cyril), which were brought by Madame. Repeated relays back and forth by Cyril, Will, and Yoann

Delivery day for the floor tiles.

were needed for unloading so many tiles. (Has there ever before existed an electrician who jumps right in to tote deliveries?) It took nearly twenty minutes, but all were stacked neatly outside the future kitchen door within easy grasp. Monsieur Roulin even loaned his battered wheelbarrow, and asked Madame Chauvin if he should assist. She advised the spry gardener to just leave it all to the young men.

Another round of decisions about the fireplace (where is my engineer husband?) and it was time to meet with Monsieur Roulin about his bill. I'd spoken with his business manager and English-speaking son, Olivier, over the weekend. Steve and I now happily knew that Parc Nationale Roulin had come at quite a bargain. I had put together his payment as had been calculated in advance. As it was raining, he and I conducted our business in the barn.

Monsieur Roulin checked his watch, and then asked if I agreed upon the time that he was finishing for the day. Of course I agreed, and he quickly made his final calculations on the back of an envelope on top of the tractor seat. The sum he presented was 35 euros less than projected. I tried to press the full amount upon him as a tip, but he vehemently protested — he would only grant me a credit instead. I told him once again that we were absolutely thrilled with the results of his efforts to spruce up this marvelous property. His reply? *C'est normal*.

Love, Kyle/Mom/Kiki

*Monsieur Roulin planting lavender along the path from
the village once utilized by the Doctor's patients.*

Cyril and the "Leeest"

I got a chance to write this on the airplane between forced conversations with my seat mate. It's been an amazing time! I would never have been able to recall the details of all these stories, and do them justice later, so I've been glad to send you these reports. It was a great outlet, and helped to keep me sane while preparing the new home. Dad and I will try to get in touch by phone soon! Anyway, here's the windup.

Dear Leigh Annie and Reid,

I was feeling a bit frantic. There is much to finish at the French Farmhouse, and my flight home was fast approaching. I called Annie for a pep talk. As usual, she was her calm and encouraging self — giving me advice for the last face-to-face with Cyril before I departed. If I haven't told you before, she and Tim have been stalwart and invaluable support throughout this entire process. From the initial visit to the property, to sending a contractor over for a structural inspection of the house and review of electrical and other reports, to conferring on the offer, and of course to sending us Cyril — they've been there every step of the way. We truly wouldn't be tackling this project without them.

As you of course know, Dad and I built our Orlando house, and have undertaken lots of remodeling. Each experience has been unique — some pleasant, and others ghastly. From my missives to you I think you can guess that this project, while hard work, has been pretty wonderful — mostly because of the people involved. Dad wryly asked when I burst into tears the night before he was leaving me solely in charge, "Are you upset because everything is going so well?" Anyway, with Steve away, I was again in need of reassurance, and Annie came through.

Armed once more with courage, I tucked my folders into the spiffy, new bag Kathy had given me, and set off down the street. I'm a pretty compulsive list maker, and both Cyril and I have come to depend on what he calls the "Leeest." Based on our daily conversations, I update them in the evenings and email them back to Cyril. When Dad left with his computer, I no longer had print capabilities, so Cyril began to do this for me in both French and English. He totes them to work the following day for us to review together.

In my remodeling experience, the homeowner usually utilizes a list to browbeat the contractor into actually accomplishing everything he's promised to do. But in working with Cyril, he often uses it to point out a nuance on an item that I hadn't thought of — perhaps the need for a piece of moulding here, or to show me loose tiles there. We also use the list to clarify our communications — he's terrified he'll misunderstand, still mortified about starting the unwanted stairway to the wine cellar.

Suffice it to say, we had a productive two-hour walk-through of every area that he, Yoann, Will, and Will's sister Vivihg were determined to improve. Yes, Will brought in his darling sister, Vivihg, (with half a head of

Exposed torchis *between the sandblasted beams.*

Will and his sister, Vivihg, standing under the newly sandblasted kitchen beams.

46

lovely chestnut hair — the other half was shaved) to stand on a ladder for four long days and scrape bits of paint left behind on the sandblasted beams. I left reassured that, while there may definitely be a few surprises when I return in May, we are in good and faithful hands, and it will be okay.

Dragging myself back to the French House to pack up for home, I shouted out my now familiar refrain to Kathy, "Where's the Scotch?!"

Love and miss you all, Mom/Kiki

Old walls and plaster were demolished by hand and then removed by Cyril in many, many wheelbarrow loads.

Part 2
Renovations and Home Furnishings

✦ ✦

September – October 2013

Back at the French Farmhouse

Well, it's been a wild few days since I returned to Fresnay! I acted as tour guide for the first two days after arriving here with our friends, before they departed for a jaunt to Brittany. They'll return next Tuesday for one night, and then they're off to Normandy, Paris, and environs. They love the French House and the village, so that's great news. They're definitely buying our share in the French House. It will be great fun to have them as neighbors after we've settled into the French Farmhouse down the street.

Dear Sweet Family,

I went to see Cyril at our French Farmhouse for the first time since our departure three months ago — he never ceases to amaze me. He's now laboring away in the TV room, leveling the floor tiles of what were previously two rooms (the doctor's waiting room and office) and are now one. This task was not easy to accomplish, as when the wall separating the two areas was removed, we discovered that the floors were two different heights by about half an inch. Cyril removed enough tiles on either side, leveled the area in between, and is now connecting the two floors.

Next, he'll turn his attention back to the pesky fireplace project. He plans to install the flue, and then brick the inside of the hearth. The old fireplace we uncovered proved to be too shallow for our needs. To extend the hearth, the mantel has to be placed a few inches out from the wall. I'd found a picture to show him, which incorporates one such fireplace, utilizing a lovely plaster design along the sides and up above the mantel to incorporate its protrusion into the room. Cyril claims that it will be easy for him to copy, so I think this issue is finally resolved. While the plaster on the fireplace dries, he will finish the other three walls in the room, and then he'll mortar and repoint the end wall, which we're leaving as exposed rock. After all this labor — voilà — the new family room will ready for the painter! Wow!

Simon, our carpenter has also arrived, and we settled an issue in the new kitchen. The windows in France seem to all open in the middle and into the room. He'd created a coffee station under such a window, which opens in and looks out onto the terrace. Now we'll be able to enjoy the view down to the river while making our morning coffee. We'd like to be able to open the window as well, but the coffee pot would be in the way. So Simon suggested that we replace what's here now with one that has a fixed glass panel at the bottom to take advantage of the view, with a window which would open above it. Now I just need to measure the coffee pot! Voilà encore!

When I returned to the French House, there was a message from our gardener's son, telling me that the Roulins had invited us over for a visit. The grounds had been beautifully maintained in our absence, and I look forward to showering lots of praise on Monsieur over refreshments at his home. (He has even removed the demolition rubble, which was piled high outside of the family room door, so that Cyril can focus on completing the work inside. This will truly be the house that Cyril, Simon, and Monsieur Roulin built.) I replied that your dad won't be here until later in the month, and I knew that he wouldn't want to miss such an occasion. I received a raincheck on the invitation.

All for now! Will keep you updated! Can't wait for you all to come and see the house for yourselves, and to stay with us in La Belle France!

Love, Mom

Remembrance Poppies in full bloom by the barn.

The artistry of joining floor tiles between two former rooms (before grouting).

The kitchen's new coffee station has a nice view of the garden.

Cyril and the bread oven

Today is a special day for our family... the day your dad was born. It was very hard being away from him on his birthday. Here's a look at what happened here without him.

Dear Sweet Kids,

Once upon a time prior to having lovely pastry shops, the French people in each community relied on a centrally located oven for their daily bread. One such ancient artifact is located in Tim and Annie's outbuilding on their country property in Belfond. The oven has an opening about 18-inches in height and width, through which bread was once inserted with a long-handled wooden paddle, while a wood fire burned brightly underneath — much like the ovens in some of our modern pizza joints.

An ancient bread oven at Annie and Tim's.

The interior of this oven is probably two-feet high, six-feet wide and six-feet deep. I'm relaying these dimensions to you for a reason, as I found Cyril crammed inside of it. He was lying on his side, scooping up the sand which had fallen down from between the bricks above him. On his head was a hat with a light, similar to one a coal miner would wear.

I'd come to see Tim (Annie is in Scotland visiting an exhibit about her ancestor, a 1920s female Arctic explorer) to view the color of the mortar on some stonework Cyril had done for them. Cyril and I have had countless conversations about the color of the mortar for the one wall in the family room, where we're leaving the stone exposed without plastering over it. After the umpteenth conversation with my pointing at an existing mortar color on the outside of our house, Cyril was still unconvinced that I'd truly made a selection. So he'd asked me to go and visit his stonework at Tim and Annie's, and to check out the color of the mortar in-between.

I drove up and parked in front of the vast stone archway which

Cyril's stone and mortar work at Annie and Tim's house.

Cyril had created. On one of her antiquing forays, Annie had acquired two huge, wooden, doors. Their installation inside of the stone arch had repurposed them as garage doors, behind which Tim parks his beloved Porsche. Of course I loved the color of the mortar Cyril had used there, which gets us back to the story of why he was gathering sand inside of the oven. He'd used this very particular brown sand, to create just the right color for the mortar in the aforementioned archway. (I forgot to ask how this material was ever discovered inside of Tim and Annie's bread oven!)

He was now collecting more of it, with Tim's permission, for the stone wall at our French Farmhouse. Cyril's wife and current helper retrieved the sand as Cyril hauled it out of the bread oven. She then sifted it in an overly large sifter, like kids use at the beach, and placed the sand inside of several buckets which were lined along the driveway. Once finished, these buckets were loaded into the back of their car in order to cart it all to the French Farmhouse. I can't make this stuff up.

Tim was nice enough to help me with a session of Cyril's paperwork, and then to fix me lunch. Afterward, I drove back to the French Farmhouse, where Cyril had already concocted a mortar sample for me, utilizing different quantities of the very special bread oven sand along with "ordinary" sand. He'd carefully laid out the mortar-pie to dry on a

Cyril in front of the exposed stone wall in the petite maison, prior to applying just the right concoction of mortar.

leftover clay tile, with its own special formula etched along the front edge. I saw several tiles laid out without samples as yet, so I asked him to please limit my choices to three. I'm sure that at least one of them will be perfect — just like the color of the mortar on the house wall, which I've been pointing to all along.

Happy Birthday, Sweetheart! Love, Kyle/Mom

Chimney sweeps in foreign lands, Cyril and his plaster, and the hunt for household items

Dear Family,

When I lived in Germany as a child, it was good luck to shake the hand of a chimney sweep. My parents frequently entertained, as my father worked as a civilian in allied missile defense alongside all of the big brass in the U.S Air Force in Wiesbaden. At one of their large soirées, a young chimney sweep, his face smeared in soot and dressed all in black, stood at the front door to greet the guests as they arrived. He was a huge hit, and left an indelible memory, as I was allowed to hang out and chat with him.

I'm sharing this story because tomorrow a chimney sweep arrives at the French Farmhouse, and then I'll see how it all works in another European country — but you can bet that I'll be shaking the hand of this chimney sweep, too. Lesley, bless her, will be on hand. She plans to come early for coffee, and after almost three weeks here alone, I'll be glad of the company — for an extrovert like me that's a loooong time!

Another visit today with Cyril at the French Farmhouse to ooh and ahhhh over the plaster work he's finished between the beams in the TV room. This week, he's progressed to the third beam. Counting thirteen all together in this room, I'm hoping that he'll be done by Thanksgiving. It's arduous work, as he scrapes away the loose plaster

After meticulous attention to detail, another example of Cyril's craftsmanship emerges.

making sure that all of the *torchis* above stays in place. Then he re-plasters the same area. On his second pass, he scrapes away any rough patches before applying the final coat. His wife then follows behind him with a wire brush, to remove any bits of plaster which may have adhered to the wood beams.

I'm sure that when Steve and I gaze up from time to time, while watching television or reading in this room, we'll remember Cyril and all his tedious efforts. I'm also fairly certain that the doctor's old patients would have difficulty recognizing his former office and w a i t i n g   r o o m . (These definitely are walls that could talk!)

In attempting to pass the time and be productive, I've been on the hunt for b a t h r o o m   t i l e s , washing machines, and dryers, as well as light fixtures and sofas. The modern

A rough coat by Cyril begins the plaster process in the kitchen.

French have interesting taste, particularly in bathrooms and light fixtures. You'd think it'd be a simple task to find small, hexagonal, white floor tiles and rectangular white subway wall tiles, with additional petite black ones to use as a border — but you'd be mistaken.

After two hours at a *magasin de carrelage* with the lovely saleswoman, Béatrice — voilà! We found what I was looking for in one of their many books of tile selections. Thank goodness for the magazine pictures I'd been toting around! Tomorrow I'll comparison shop at another store, but I'm hoping to do business with the very patient Béatrice.

As to finding simple light fixtures for our bathrooms — there's not a chance. Instead, the light fixtures here resemble twisted aliens with strange heads that look as if they'd bite. I haven't given up the hunt, but you may visit and wonder, "Why did she pick that one?" Then I'll hope that you'll remember this story.

Missing you — really! Counting the days until your Dad arrives. The local "Dirty Old Man" who keeps propositioning me is starting to look good!

Love, Kyle/Mom

To think that these are examples of the more "simple" light fixtures from which I had to choose.

Road trip,
Commotion at the French Farmhouse,
and a dinner date

Dear Family,

Today, as I whizzed past ancient Normandy churches and hanging pots profuse with brilliant flowers, I recalled a snippet mentioned to Steve and to me by our friend, Tom. He'd commented that, in our little French corner of the world, each village is even lovelier than the last. As I rolled past plump livestock, and the heads of this year's sunflowers now brown and drooping in the fields, I held similar thoughts about the passing landscape.

One of the best things about rural France is that you can just get in the car and drive — rarely is there traffic and there's seldom a stoplight (I encountered three today while traveling a distance of over forty miles). The only hazard is the ubiquitous French tailgater, but you can usually just relax and enjoy the scenery.

Radio Nostalgique, blasting a mixture of Motown, Beatles, Disco, and French Cabaret per their promo, kept me company as I headed for Fontaine-Daniel, a little village which has a toile manufacturing industry. Once there, I loved the fabrics but not the prices, so I'll probably stick to Calico Corners — well, maybe a sofa pillow — but the drive was spectacular. The weather was clear with temperatures in the mid-seventies.

I returned to Fresnay in time to meet with John, Lesley's husband and our plumber, to discuss the new master bathroom. As we are now converting the doctor's offices into our kitchen and family room, we are able to transform Madame's old kitchen into our master bath. Due diligence had me visiting additional tile showrooms to comparison shop for the plain bathroom tiles I've been seeking.

Each time I declined to consider the displays of aqua striped tiles with companion polka dots, or the large murals of lavender flowers. I was told, *"Non,"* whenever I pulled out my magazine pictures of traditional bathrooms. So it was back to Beatrice with her musical laughter at our combined French and English, and the master bathroom tiles have finally been ordered!

Beatrice protested when I selected the floor grout in gray, but I'm old enough to know better than to select white. I don't intend to spend my time, or Lesley's, scrubbing between tiny, white, octagonal floor tiles. She discounted the order 20 percent, and then pretended not to believe my age — a great saleswoman!

After paying my deposit, I had just enough time to hit the Thursday market in Alençon for fruits and veggies before grabbing lunch at one of our favorite restaurants. After a ten euro feast of fresh trout and roasted root vegetables, I stopped by a marvelous patisserie to pick out a dessert, along with some of their pizza for my evening meal. Then I headed back to the French House and to complete chaos.

I was just finishing up a translation at the kitchen table for the painter and waiting for my lucky chimney sweep, when our neighbor, British Peter, arrived unannounced. He had to tell me all about his lengthy drive to and from Austria with his wife — who lives separately from him in England. His unburdening was not to be denied, so I poured coffee for him and for Lesley, who'd also arrived.

Conversation was one-sided until our chimney sweep, Didier, turned up. (Although I tried twice, he wouldn't shake my hand, protesting that he was just too sooty!) I ushered both Peter and Didier out of the door just as the painter, Andre, arrived. He and I went over the to-do lists for both houses, while Lesley chimed in with the translation of sticky words like semi-gloss.

The day ended on a pitch-black road in the pouring rain, with the aforementioned octogenarian neighbor behind the wheel. We had a lovely time eating fish and chips at Peter's favorite new restaurant in St. Paul de Gautier. And I learned not to try out a perfume sample before jumping into a car. My date described it as "not so great." This from a man whose gaseous dog — fed a consistent diet of sausages and pâté — was riding along with us in the back seat. Tomorrow, there's a *brocante* fair I'll attend with Tim, and then I'll make preparations for Dad's arrival at long last. I'd better get some sleep.

Miss you all. Until later.

Love, Kyle/Mom

British Peter and his trusty pal, George.

An inaugural fire, yet another masonry consultation, and a walk on the beach

Dear Family,

Yesterday was a banner day in the life of the new fireplace at the French Farmhouse. First, Annie and Tim surprised me with a lovely pair of antique andirons — a perfect fit for the hearth. Then we watched with cautious anticipation as Cyril ceremoniously lit a fire inside the fireplace opening (complete with hearthstone). As smoke curled and flowed directly upward inside the chimney, we all clapped and cheered. A beaming Cyril executed a little bow. With hugs all around, and after consultations and opinions on paint and drapery samples, we naturally went off to celebrate with lunch and wine!

Inaugural flames in the almost finished fireplace.

As I last told you, the ever talented Simon will provide the necessary masonry work prior to the roofing insulation job. We spent some time today examining chimneys, looking at the existing chimney pots, and deciding exactly what should be done. The outside wall to the *petite maison* also needs some repair, and we discussed the color options for the mortar. Simon knows that our desire is to leave the old character of the house intact with any new work that is done. So, like Cyril, he plans to conjure up a custom mix. Looking at the ancient walls surrounding the rest of the house, I believe there is enough masonry work to partially provide for Simon's retirement, and to substantially deplete ours!

Today I joined our caretaker, Lesley, and another of her friends and clients, Jenny, for a jaunt around the lake at Sillé Beach. You may remember my previous story about Easter lunch there, which Lesley hosted for all of her "peeps." She truly acts as our Mother Hen, looking after us whether absent or present in Fresnay. Today was the latter, as the ever thoughtful Lesley knows I'm sojourning alone at the Bourgneuf House. Her aim was to provide me with alternative companionship to contractors, and the local Dirty Old Man, who keeps urging me to flee (or, in his case, limp away) with him.

I'd met today's companion, Jenny, during my brief stint of French lessons at the home of a lady in the neighboring village of Saint Léonard des Bois. When our English instructor mispronounced *des États-Unis d'Amérique*, which I do know, I decided against continuing with her lessons. So, it was nice to once again see Jenny, a former prima ballerina in London, who, as you would expect, is a graceful and lovely woman.

Like Lesley, Jenny is an expat from England. There are quite a few Brits here, enjoying the tranquility of French country life, despite their bloody history of territorial disputes. The weather was gorgeous, and Jenny, Lesley, and I had a jolly time walking with their three dogs around the quite large and lovely lake, and then enjoying coffee afterwards. How nice to be thought of and accepted in this way, when I am far away from family and my Orlando friends.

Love, Kyle/Mom

Mother would approve

Dear Family,

I learned to bargain literally at my mother's (Mimi's) knee. With the favorable exchange rate of four-to-one, my mother bought up as many of the treasures of post-war Germany that she could find. In her Mississippi accent, with me (her five- to eight-year-old) acting as interpreter, she drove a hard bargain. She'd wear her victims down until the desired object was hers.

Today's *brocante* fair was a test of my Mother's tutelage, and I hope I did her proud. As Tim and I stood under umbrellas looking at the chandelier and sconces we'd spied before the rain began, which were now covered by plastic, I asked for the price "ensemble" and offered half. Since the vendor knew his prospects were poor in today's weather, we walked away with Tim toting the chandelier, and me carting the wall sconces — with his earlier purchase of two red chili peppers peeking out of his back pocket. We now possess a light fixture for one of the guest bedrooms, reading lights for the master bedroom, and a memorable story.

Tim with his red peppers.

We lunched at a lovely auberge in Domfront, while

waiting for the Antiquités du Donjon to open for the afternoon. There we picked up an old beveled and framed mirror, as well as a tripod occasional table, both of which had been on my list to find. After tea to recoup, and a look at items in Tim and Annie's barn that they may want to part with, I left for Fresnay, where I found Cyril along with his entire family hard at work in the house. The gardener had finally gotten his car out of the shop, and had removed the last pile of rubble from the middle of the TV room. And, our chosen formula for the mortar had been made and was being applied to the stone wall — except it was too late in the day to see what I thought of the color!

Love, Kyle/Mom

Hollyhocks in bloom along the driveway.

Bells, a reunion, and hazelnut trees

Dear Kids,

I love the sound of church bells. In our little French village, they chime to announce the hour, proclaim services and celebrations, and to inexplicably (yet nonetheless exuberantly) announce something at exactly 6:20 p.m. every evening.

The book I'm currently reading, *The Discovery of France* by Graham Robb, says, "Bells marked the tribal territory and gave it voice." It goes on to say, "When the bell was being cast by a traveling founder, villagers added heirlooms to the metal — old plates, coins, and candlesticks — and turned it into the embodiment of the village soul." This morning, the symbol of Fresnay's spirit signaled to me that the time was finally at hand to collect my soulmate from the train station.

It was a grand reunion. Something about standing on a French train platform on a foggy morning while waiting for a loved one felt very "film noir," except that I wished fervently for better hair. Your dad said he picked out my feet from the sea of shoes — all that was visible as the train whizzed past before braking. Tracing back, we'd discovered that it was our longest separation since 1970, and although we had a multitude of excellent reasons for this one, we made a pact not to intentionally repeat the experience. Both strong-willed, we are at times obstinate with each other, but rarely at the same time. Ours, we know, is a fortunate love story.

None of the potential scenarios which had played out in my head as I descended the "treacherous" steps to the basement for laundry, or drove through malfunction junction, had occurred. I was not sniffed out and found by British Peter's dog, George, days after lying with a broken leg on the basement floor. I hadn't lost my car keys, my cash, had a major appliance erupt, or even received a parking ticket. The French House was not lying in smoldering ash, as I'd always remembered to unplug the non-automatic, switch-off coffee pot. And renovations at the French Farmhouse, while still resembling a home under siege, had progressed well. I was ready to exhale, lean on a familiar and much loved shoulder, and have someone else change the odd, French light bulb.

We celebrated with a visit to the new house, and your dad showed sufficient appreciation to Cyril for his heroic efforts on our behalf. After harvesting hazelnuts and walnuts from beneath newly discovered trees, and in between bites of ripe pears, figs, apples, and grapes from the property, we sat on the terrace sipping wine. The church bells chimed their regular music, and all seemed right in the world. So glad to have your Dad back!

Love you guys, Mom

Rendezvous at the train station in Le Mans.

A simpler life

Dad asked me tonight how we could still have such a long list of things to do — after we've already achieved so much! My response was that it could have something to do with the fact that we undertook the renovation and redecorating of a centuries-old French Farmhouse! That was when we decided to take a day off from all of the projects.

Dear Sweet Family,

It's fungi celebration time in France. Mushrooms are sprouting on damp, forest floors all over the region. After a whirlwind week of construction accomplishments, Dad and I decided to partake in the excitement of the 61st Annual Mushroom Fête in Belleme, a town forty miles northeast of Fresnay. However, we first needed some provisions, so we ventured a little further north to Mortagne du Perche. The region is famous for their sturdy draft horses, known as Percherons.

A lively Saturday market provided a bounty from which to choose. Pulling our trusty cart behind us, we loaded up on aged cheeses, marinated olives, farm fresh eggs, and butter — as well as lush, ripe tomatoes, nectarines, plums, and melons. Once fully stocked, we headed toward Belleme, pausing for a lunch featuring the

Steve, trundling home with fresh produce from a favorite market in Mortagne du Perche.

stars of the season. Even Dad's pear au gratin dessert contained mushrooms!

At the fête, you may choose to attend lectures on mushrooms (in French), visit exhibits, or be instructed through guided tours in the forest. Since both Lesley and Tim have offered to take us on mushroom hunts, we opted for the exhibits. The first unexpected display we encountered was of delicately dyed yarns — their soft colors garnered from a wide variety of mushrooms.

Dozens of edible fungi, probably half of those to be found on the forest floor, were displayed accompanied by a picture of a knife and fork. The other half shown in the exhibit were either toxic or fatal if ingested, duly tagged with a doctor's bag or skull and crossbones. Since it's difficult to discern the good from the bad in the forest sans pictures, posters on the wall advised us to take any of these found delicacies to the local pharmacist for identification before sampling.

Inedible mushrooms on display with an informative warning.

Prior to departing Belleme, a lucky find in a local fabric shop resulted in just the right silk material to reupholster my mother's old French chairs. Heading south, we located the Routes des Brocantes, a road dotted with antique stores of varying quality. All together we drove about 120 miles, encountering only three traffic lights and lots of gorgeous scenery. Plugging in the best shops on our GPS to return to another day, we headed home to watch the sunset once again from the terrace.

Looking down at the yard near the woodshed, we noticed a new sprout of mushrooms in the grass. They will definitely require identification from our helpful, local pharmacist. For life's simpler pleasures, this is definitely an entertaining place in which to live.

Love, Mom

This ancient-looking woodshed is one of the many exterior structures at the centuries-old French Farmhouse.

More than sustenance, two steps forward — one step back, and a flue

Loved talking to you both this week. The saga continues here.

Dear Sweet, Grown Kids,

I have to say a word or two about the meal we just enjoyed. After collecting more necessary construction items at the third self-service, big-box store in a row, my spirits were flagging. (You will never miss customer service before your time, but I can still remember Mr. Harper at Harper's paints in Orlando. He could mix the perfect paint color from a dog-eared magazine picture I'd bring to him.)

Dad chose to stop at the Auberge des Hunaudieres in Le Mans for sustenance. The special starter of the day was a soufflé of Coquille St. Jacques accompanied by a cream and chives mixture poured into the center. My main course was pot-au-feu with duck, and Dad enjoyed beef medallions wrapped in bacon, accompanied by asparagus and lima beans served over creamy polenta — all for the gigantic sum of thirteen euros each.

My nostalgia for Mr. Harper is not without reason. Two of the paint colors, we'd so lovingly chosen and painted on white cardboard stock in Florida, did not translate as expected onto the walls in Fresnay. The blush color we chose for the parlor resembles bubble gum or a nursery room — the painter's comment was, *"pour bébé"* — and the sunny yellow in the kitchen clashes with the pink cast in the cabinets, so we're poring over additional paint chip colors.

We may have found the hue we're aiming for in the parlor, and we've painted a trial patch on the wall — fingers crossed. Meanwhile, the definitive step forward is the removal of three stories of orange wallpaper from the foyer, and all the way up the three-story stairwell. Already we see the gray color of the encaustic tile pattern in the foyer leap out with the touch of gray wall paint (that one seems to be working) and white trim.

John has been working furiously in the master bath, and we've been just as frantically trying to collect up all the elements required for his task (see first paragraph above). However, finding the right bathroom light fixtures still eludes us.

Meanwhile, Cyril continues to plaster walls, but at least all of the areas between the beams in the TV room are finally finished. We ooh and ahh appropriately over the mortar on the stone wall as it dries and the final color emerges.

The fireplace is also receiving Cyril's and our attention once again. The flue, a handcrafted, counterbalanced fire door, which can be opened and closed with one finger, was duly obtained and paid for last night at a metallurgist's shop. Once again, Dad tried to impart the American expression, "Cash on the barrelhead," to the owner, who'd asked to be paid in euros. Cyril translated the owner's query back to us, "Did he mean that Americans dip their money in a beer barrel?" I told him that some things just don't translate well, and to give it up.

Love, Mom

Paint and fabric samples for the French Farmhouse. (All of those magazines from Annie came in handy!)

French errands, and separation by uncommon accents

It has been nonstop this week — orchestrating subcontractors. Happy birthday to Campbell! Here is a small update.

Dear Family,

I never thought I'd travel down a backcountry road with a French painter discussing the results of his recent colonoscopy, but then again there have been quite a few surprises lately. Dad and I spent the better part of this week motoring to Caen, Le Mans and Alençon to collect supplies: sinks, cabinets, faucets, wood doors, etc. for subcontractors — including today's trip for paint supplies. The washers, dryers, and love seats (coordinating with paint chips) have been selected and purchased with all upcoming delivery dates duly noted. Shopkeepers and sales clerks have been generous, as well as patient, with *les Américains*.

Interaction with either of the painters who speak

Andre, our French painter extraordinaire.

in local French patois (not the pronunciation on my French language CDs), along with a plumber and carpenter with varying English accents, has been challenging, to say the least. And let's not forget Cyril — whose speech, like the man himself (who is still plastering walls) defies categorizing. All is slowly evolving at the French Farmhouse on rue du Clos de Paris. A real home, where we can comfortably welcome family and friends, is emerging from the chaos.

We look forward to the arrival of two such dear friends tomorrow. We're desperately hoping that Paul and Mary Ann, who are staying with us for a few days at the French House following their hiking trip in the Lot Valley, will save us from ourselves. We're due a respite from house errands and decisions — hah!

Love, Mom

John and Simon enjoying a deserved break from their labors.

Problems, solutions, and friendship

Dear Family,

There's something quite wonderful about synergism and teamwork. Prior to our purchase of the house, lead paint was reported in two small areas. One area cited was the baseboards in part of the foyer, which are currently slated for painting. I had the lead paint report inside of my folder, but had been so confounded choosing colors, that I'd neglected to alert the painters. Cyril, however, did remember. And Simon, who is brilliantly replacing windows and repairing woodwork at the house, jumped to the rescue. He will quickly change out the old baseboards with new wood, and the painters will remain on track.

Meanwhile, Dad and I had not so brilliantly decided to try out a patch of the just purchased paint from one of the huge two-gallon containers, and were dismayed to watch our pale mushroom-gray color bloom green on the foyer wall. The next morning, with translated note in hand, we informed Andre of our alarm. Had we acquired the wrong paint color — and lots of it? Andre patiently explained that even though the paint had been mixed at the store the day we tried it out, it had settled. Mixed properly, the true color appeared — duh! His assistant, sanding walls from a ladder perched above us, looked down on the scene as if to say, "Civilians!" (I still think it's a little more greenish than it should be, but the color is nice.)

Our international crew of craftsmen welcomed its ʹsixth member to the French Farmhouse today. Les is a burly Scotsman who brings brings yet another accent into the mix. He's installing additional electrical wiring for the new master bath, and it's now far enough along so that John can install the tile we collected from the *magasin de carrelage*. After peering at the tile for so long in my magazine picture, and in Beatrice's books, it was nice to finally see the real thing.

Paul and Mary Ann have indeed added some frivolity to our days, with pool matches at Au Bon Coin and lots of great conversations. They are cheering us on, and seem content to be here during this time of chaos. We have just completed a stroll around town, and are all sprawled comfortably by the fire back at the French House. (And Dad is actually roasting chestnuts!) We'll check in at the Cafe du Commerce later on to discover if our earlier two euro horse racing bet paid off, and

74

then enjoy aperitifs with Canadian Peter and Lynda this evening. All's well that ends well — another fine day in La Belle France.

Love, Mom

Mary Ann and Paul visiting the French Farmhouse construction zone.

Proprietor John Rene readies Au Bon Coin for another day. Located on the corner of "Malfunction Junction," it's a local favorite for aperitifs and a game of pool.

A singer, a launderer, and a temper tantrum

Dear Family,

Rock star by night, installer of snakelike wires in our master bath by day. Such is the resume of our electrician, Les, who is also the lead singer in a local band. Shortly after he gave us a demo of his music today, we parked our car outside the bathroom where he was working and "rocked out" with his CD at full volume. Les seemed to be pleased, and amused, by our antics.

Then, as we were leaving, Andre asked if we were going to keep

If our wiring reminds anyone of a mixing board at a Led Zeppelin concert, there's good reason for for that.

the sheers, which had been hanging in the large staircase windows until he'd taken them down in preparation for painting. I looked them over and pronounced them fine, as it was one less thing to replace. Andre's response was, in that case, he would take them home to be washed before hanging them back up for us. Only in France!

However, lest you think all here is Kumbaya, a slight kerfuffle ensued when Cyril got his nose out of joint with John. Dipping into supplies at the other end of the house, John apparently invaded his space. Cyril, behind on his "leeest" and tired from laboring seven days a week, left early in a huff. We're hoping some rest will soothe his artistic temperament, and we're positive that he'll air his grievances with us tomorrow. It's a big house, but obviously not large enough to contain all of these disparate personalities.

Meanwhile, Dad and I continue our elusive search for the "right" paint color in the kitchen. We may, voilà, have stumbled on it today. We'll inspect the dried samples of paint on the walls tomorrow, and let you know. Wish it was as easy as the off-white trim paint which we picked out in the car on our way to the paint store. It's now called "70 mph White."

Love, Mom

*Les, the "Electric Rocker" when he came to help
spread a newly delivered truckload of gravel.*

A very enterprising young man, and English/French zones

Dear Leigh Anne and Reid,

When I told you about our visit from Didier, the town chimney sweep, I forgot to mention that he's also the village propane gas distributor, as well as the local wine merchant. Tonight we stopped by his "cave" to restock, and he invited us to share some wine with him as it was the hour for aperitifs.

Opening a nice bottle of Sauvignon Blanc, Didier poured a glass for each of us. Then he began to relate his story. It seems that this enterprising young man is not only the purveyor of wine, gas, firewood, and the cleaner of chimneys in Fresnay, but he's also the owner of a pub in Alençon, the landlord of several apartment buildings, as well as the bookkeeper for his wife's dance lesson business, which has 300-plus students.

Our village's jack-of-all-trades, Didier.

It's his choice to work all the time, he tells us, as his goal is to retire and travel the world in seven years' time. He went on to say that he loves his job selling wine because people come to see him when they are either happy and want to celebrate — or in need of a gift of wine to make someone else happy! There's a great slogan in there somewhere, but I was afraid if I mentioned it, this extraordinary entrepreneur would add the distribution of bumper stickers to his long list of endeavors. We bid him *bonne soirée*, departing with our purchases and the remaining contents of our shared bottle of wine.

The English zone, where John labored away on our new master bath.

Cyril returned to the house today, and as expected he let me know about his unhappiness with John. Dad disappeared into another part of the house, while I soothed Cyril's feelings and told him how sorry I was that he'd been upset. Later in the day, Dad bought another outdoor water hose for John to use on his side of the house. He intends to tell John in the morning that Cyril's side is off limits — and that's when I plan to disappear.

Love, Mom

The French zone, where Cyril transformed the kitchen and the television room.

A neighbor, and a solution

Beside the fact that Cyril is still plastering the new family room wall, here's what has been happening lately.

Dear Family,

Down the street, the two transvestite owners finally sold their house to an interesting woman named Martine, who knocked on our door the other day to introduce herself. During our subsequent chat, she told me that she'd entirely redone her house, and had furnished it with items leftover from her recently closed antique store — which she'd operated for 23 years in Deauville. She then invited us over to have aperitifs along with her boyfriend, Jean Louis. Dad and I had an opportunity to view the transformed home, and to visit with the seemingly happy couple. She has stunning taste, and all was absolutely lovely.

Dad then saw Martine a couple days later on the street, and he stopped to speak with her. She commented on the German sports car we had rented, and he in turn inquired as to how she liked her Citroen. Her reply to him was, "It's a French car — not very good — like French men."

Today, a lively discussion ensued over humidity and the sticking of paint to the wall. Dad and I listened patiently (sort of) while our painter and plumber discussed what was needed to remedy the situation. Andre was veering down the path of renting an expensive dehumidifier, when Dad jumped in to say that a couple of inexpensive, plug-in heaters should do the trick. So the plumber went off to purchase heaters for the painter to use, as he needed some supplies as well.

That solved, I nailed down the time tomorrow when Andre and I would drive once again to Alençon, to buy more paint in the decided upon colors for the remaining downstairs rooms. He may elaborate further upon his four marriages and six children on the drive. As he understated to me on our previous run for paint — his life is rather complicated.

Love, Mom

His Honor, euros dispensed, future coiffures, and adieu

A week-plus at home and I'm almost caught up — after experiencing daylight-saving time twice. Here's my wrap-up.

Dear Family,

There's a lovely view down to the Sarthe River out of the mayor's office window. British Peter, Dad, and I lined up like ducklings in front of the *maire's* desk. Laid out before him was a packet of pictures Dad had snapped of the current facade of the *grande maison*. Included was a pencil drawing I'd created of the proposed look, complete with a picture of new shutters along with a paint swatch for *les volets* .

Rumor has it that once upon a time in France and elsewhere in Europe, homeowners were taxed according to how many windows they had in their homes. Thus began a widespread tax dodge of blocking up existing windows. There are three such areas on the *grande maison*. I'd hit upon an idea to put closed shutters on each of these eyesores, alongside working shutters on the remaining windows. The idea is to hide the fact that any windows were blocked, and to recreate symmetry on the front of the house. This was the day we were to discover what "The Decider" thought of the plan.

The plans we submitted to "The Decider" for disguising the blocked-off windows.

The packet was viewed, and a nod of approval emanated from His Honor. A conversation then began regarding the paperwork, which must be filed with the town's Architectural Committee. These papers will in turn be sent to French Government officials in charge of Fresnay's designation as La Petites Cités de Caractère to complete our request. We trooped out afterward, happy in the knowledge that our plans have been blessed, along with Peter's offer to assist us in filling out the pertinent forms. Dad volunteered to shepherd this task, as I had checks and euros to dispense before our departure in two day's time — along with a hairdresser to interview.

The day before leaving, Dad and I met with all the subcontractors for the French Farmhouse: Simon the carpenter, John the plumber, Sylvain the electrician (Les' electrical work was complete) Andre and Eric the painters, and of course, Cyril. All seems to be near completion (Cyril) and progressing (all the rest). Our indispensable Lesley was left in charge of postdated checks for the yet to be completed work, and receipts for items not yet delivered or picked up — washers, dryers, sofas, and the remaining tile *plinthe*. Monsieur Roulin arrived to pick up his funds for estimated work in the garden through next May, with promises of a blossoming and fruitful yard upon our return.

I'd had my meeting with a recommended hairdresser, Romain, in LeMans, bringing along the formula supplied by his Orlando counterpart. He assured me that he could touch up my graying hair next summer without dyeing it the ubiquitous eggplant color so often seen on local French heads. After some last minute repairs by Simon at the French House we shared with our friends, we were ready for our flights home.

Love, Mom

Daisies brightening up one of the outbuildings.

Part 3
The Move!

✦ ✦ ✦

May – June 2014

A death march, a chihuahua, and an arrival

On our return to Fresnay, Dad and I realized how fortunate we are to have such hard working, competent, and trustworthy help in restoring the house on rue du Clos de Paris. Here are some highlights from our first day back.

Dear Family,

In our quest to return to France at the end of April, we survived three attempts at takeoff from Orlando International Airport. Mechanical failure, an untimely thunderstorm, and the timing out of our crew had us deplaning twice — but a new crew and our third taxi down the runway was the charm. We finally hit the pillows after midnight at a hotel near Dulles for an unplanned overnight stay sans luggage — and we could only dream that the next day would finally take us to our destination. It did.

Exhausted and hungry, we drove our rental car from the Le Mans train station to our favorite little stop in the village of La Bazoge. Spying an open brasserie, we decided on sustenance over provisions, and once inside we placed two orders of the plat du jour. At that point, a young woman, adorned with a leopard print hand bag and holding an aging chihuahua, breezed in and sat beside us. So starved were we that even when the pet regurgitated onto the floor next to our table (having adoringly been fed a portion of her owner's charcuterie appetizer) it failed to stint our appetites.

Straggling into Fresnay and driving at last by the French Farmhouse, we noticed the open gates signaling workmen inside. Too tired to investigate, we fell into an exhausted sleep at the French House. Later that day, refreshed from our naps, we ventured down the street to peek at the progress since our last visit in October. Receiving pictures and updates through emails and phone calls had kept us apprised of the scope of the work being accomplished, but we couldn't wait another minute to see it all for ourselves.

Dad and I surveyed the beautiful view from the terrace, along with the results of Monsieur Roulin's toil in the gardens. Bright splashes of red climbing roses and lavender wisteria caught our attention. The latter hung from wires which now extended around the side of the first outbuilding. The fruit trees appeared trimmed and healthy, and the rose garden lush. Purple and white lilac blossoms swayed in full glory from their branches. Blue and white flowers we've yet to identify stood in profuse abundance inside multiple flower beds surrounding the house, alongside the last remaining pink and candy-striped tulips. The bright green lawn and shrubs had been manicured in anticipation of our arrival. We couldn't have been more pleased.

Mr. Roulin's handiwork on the outbuildings at Clos de Paris.

Holding our breath, we crept inside to see how the paint swatches had translated into the present, colorful rooms. Andre had done an absolutely masterful job removing layers of wallpaper, repairing plaster walls, sanding trim, and painting surfaces. Moving from room to room we looked at each other and smiled, extremely happy with the results. The "Nun's Blush," as our friend Tom has christened the rosy hue in the parlor and in the kitchen, looked just right with the deep, white crown moulding and kitchen cabinets. The mellow gold in the family room appeared to be the perfect selection on the walls, alongside the old wood beams and mantel. (After all the efforts and decisions made on the fireplace, it looked as if it has always belonged in the room.) Along with the paint work in these rooms, Andre had completed the wallpaper removal in all of the bedrooms. Now these walls stood ready to receive their new colors.

Having duly admired the painting progress, we moved on to look at the floors. Along with cleaning plaster dust from all the windows and surfaces, Lesley and her ladies had been hard at work pulling up rug squares which had formerly hidden the encaustic tiles in the parlor. They had cleaned the geometric and

Cyril's tile floor in the TV room before wall painting, and the fireplace flue completed, as pictured in the magazine page taped above the hearth.

circular mosaic patterns on the floor to restore their 18th century splendor, and it looked fabulous. And Cyril had recently returned to clean the clay tiles, which he'd so lovingly laid in the kitchen and TV room. It was really grand to find these rooms completed.

Peering into the unfinished master bath, we approved of John's fine handiwork with the white ceramic tiles and black border, and we came to a decision on how to complete the design around the opening to the shower. Along the way, we admired Simon's handiwork. He'd matched the existing crown moulding, which had been missing on one portion of the master bedroom wall. He'd also removed (from the corner of the front foyer) the remains of what had once been the old doctor's partitioned toilet area (for his patients). The roofers, recommended by Monsieur Roulin, had come and gone. They'd put new insulation in the *petite maison* attic, and the ancient roof tiles were now free of moss. Outside once again, we admired Simon's beautiful work on the repointed chimneys. All in all, there had been an abundance of wonderful progress during our absence.

Happy and still tired, we gave the view one last glance and returned to the French House for a fire in the fireplace, a glass of wine, and the writing of many thank you emails. We still have much to do, but even more has been accomplished by all of the wonderful people we have working here. Until next time.

Love, Mom and Dad

All hands (and knees) on deck

Dear Family,

There's been a flurry of activity at the French Farmhouse this week! We arrived there today to find Lesley and two of her helpers on their hands and knees scrubbing floors. They've since polished the uncovered armoires, waxed the fireplace mantel, washed the windows, and cleaned plaster dust from every nook and crevice. We know we'll be swiping at this fine, white powder for weeks to come, but the ladies have given us a great head start. Poor Andre has been a good sport about having his painting supplies moved around to make way for the cleanup. We still haven't heard from the shippers, except to learn that everything has safely arrived in France. But it looks as though we may be miraculously ready to receive the furnishings — if and when they do appear!

Our number one carpenter, Simon, has replaced all the opaque glass with clear panes in the doctor's former offices. They all sparkle due to the labors of our

Sherry and Lesley scrubbing paint off the old clay tiles in the new master bedroom.

cleaning crew, so we are reveling in the splendid views outside to the rose garden and down to the river below. Simon also finished framing in the front foyer. The doctor's partitioned, pink, potty room, which had been located there, is now (thankfully) a distant memory.

Having purchased all the remaining paint, Andre is finishing up the master bedroom downstairs, and he will start painting upstairs tomorrow. Unfortunately, John has run twenty pieces short of the white subway tiles he needs to finish the master bathroom (another trip to the tile shop) and it will take three weeks for the new order to arrive! Along with helping us to move furniture and radiators, provide translation, and introduce us to a used car dealer, John has also addressed this problem. He will tile everything except a portion of the outside of the shower, so that we can still move in (and use the bathroom) on schedule.

Meanwhile, Sylvain, the last electrician who worked at the house, is too occupied to come and hang light fixtures for us. So Andre brought in his friend, Petit Thierry, a very short Frenchman with a serious attitude. He studied our needs and promised to show up bright and early on Monday. Reassured that he's a certified electrician, we know it'll be lovely to pull out the light fixtures, which are stashed in cupboards, and to have something other than plain wires and bulbs hanging from the ceilings.

With the TV room cleaned, Dad and I couldn't wait any longer to unwrap the love seats and the coffee table we'd purchased in France last October. We plopped down on the sofas, calling dibs on the one situated with the best outdoor views... this to be decided! Gathering up receipts and *factures*, we returned to the French House to write checks and dispense euros. Your dad, blessed with boundless energy, has now ventured off to Brico Depot to buy floor mats, while I take a moment to breathe deeply — and to write to you!

"Hi" to Campbell and Margo!

Love you all, Mom

Tractor Maintenance, a family album, and a gift of honey

Dear Family,

How remarkable it is to have the services of Monsieur Roulin. As reported, the grounds at the French Farmhouse have grown lush under his spectacular care. Because he'd more than earned our faith in him, we paid Monsieur in advance last fall. He'd prepared a list of pruning and other tasks he proposed to accomplish during our absence. We knew by then that he'd go above and beyond tending to the gardens (which he has done) and it would be far easier to handle payment in this manner than to mail him checks from the United States. He claimed that he'd never been paid before in advance, and that he was honored by our faith in him.

Yesterday was the day we finally met up again since our return to France. We lavished Monsieur Roulin with praise as we reviewed his accomplishments. As expected, he'd more than completed his list — with an added caveat. He reported that he'd transported our riding tractor to his farm to grease and oil it for maintenance purposes, and he was concerned that he hadn't previously listed that task. It was definitely more than okay with us. As we thanked him profusely once again, he gave his standard reply, "*C'est normal.*"

During our evening trip down the street to check on the progress made that day, we discovered that one of our worker bees had begun to pull up the old rug squares in the master bedroom, which had been left in place until the painting was complete. We're not sure whom to thank, but I guess someone else is as impatient as we are to make progress. Dad is down there now tugging up the rest of them, and utilizing his hot-gun tool to attack the remaining glue on the clay tiles underneath. Only he could relish tackling such a task! (He got it all up!)

During yesterday's house inspection, our neighbor, Claudine, came calling while lugging a large canvas bag. Her parcel revealed a scrapbook, which had been lovingly assembled by her great aunt — who, in 1971, along with Claudine's great uncle, had stayed at the Clos de Paris house for the entire year. Her great aunt had put together memorabilia, along with many beautiful watercolors of the house and grounds (one of which is on the cover of this book) which were painted by her great uncle, Roger Planson during their stay.

Claudine is a lovely woman of a certain age, who speaks in constant streams of French. We managed to comprehend the gist of most of her conversation, and her album certainly helped! It was great fun to share some history about the French Farmhouse, as well as of the village of Fresnay. (To our delight, she later made us a gift of one of her Great Uncle's watercolors of the French Farmhouse.)

Watercolors of Fresnay and Clos de Paris, painted by Roger Planson. The fourth piece in his series is featured on this book's cover.

Sunday, Dad and I took a walk between raindrops to feed the town sheep and goats at the top of the town. We ambled back down the hill to feed a neighboring donkey, dubbed "Dennis" by British Peter, who also keeps him fed with snacks. Dennis brays when he spies Dad, and Dad has been known to bray back in response. They seem to have a special affinity for one another — but it might just be the proffered carrots.

Two of the village sheep and Dennis, our favorite local farm animal.

As we strolled back down our street, our neighbor, Guy, jumped out from his recessed doorway. He presented us with a container of his *"miel de printemps"* collected from one of the beehives he maintains at his farm outside of town. He advised us to eat it with salted butter, as the combination spread on French bread is exquisite. We relayed the recent spotting of an insect swarm buzzing over our lilac trees, and Guy assures us that he could establish a beehive on our grounds. As both Dad and Reid have bee and wasp allergies, we'll probably pass on his kind offer. We waved goodbye as Guy is planning to return to his Paris home tonight after a last stop at his farm. But, he says that if we spot his car tomorrow, it will be because he's been punctured by his friendly bees!

This week will hopefully bring the electrician and the movers, so we're fortifying ourselves tonight with escargot from Auberge des Peintres — our favorite restaurant in Saint-Ceneri. Rumor has it there's a new chef. We hope not, but if so, fingers crossed he's as excellent as the last one. We'll let you know.

Love, Mom

Steve and Guy all geared up for another honey hunt.

A cuckoo bird, light fixtures, and word from the movers

Fortified by a delicious dinner the night before — yes, the new chef is very good — we're ready for another day of pre-move preparation. Here's the latest from Fresnay.

Dear Family,

There's an actual cuckoo bird outside the house here, flying back and forth. We've heard him make his definitive calls throughout this past week, and we're wondering if he is trying to tell us something!

With such a lush backyard at the shared home, it's no wonder that cuckoo bird spent so much time there.

Unlike electricity, which flows with the flip of a switch, French electricians are not as reliable. Petit Thierry, our fourth electrician, seems to be up to completing the task that the other three started and left unfinished. He did arrive bright and early this morning, and most of the light fixtures downstairs are now hanging where they belong. As he admired the newly installed lights, Andre remarked, "We say in France, it looks like night and day." I assured him that we English speakers often make that same remark!

Our French shipping agent finally contacted us today. Due to two French bank holidays during the first part of May, customs has not yet cleared our container. He's hopeful to have it pass through later today with a tentative delivery date for Wednesday at 9:00 a.m. I'm equally thrilled and terrified. Although Andre, bless him, has managed to finish painting all the upstairs bedroom ceilings as of today. He'll just have to finish those walls around the furnishings — if we can place them out of his way!

Wish us luck this week, and that the cuckoo bird is wrong!

Love, Mom

Petit Thierry hanging a light fixture in the newly finished family room.

Mission accomplished!

Dear Family,

Yesterday was D-Day at the French Farmhouse — EVERYTHING was delivered, and not one item was damaged or broken — not even my great grandfather's, grandfather clock. Incredible! Lesley had thought ahead to request reserved space in the closest parking lot from the mayor's office for the large moving truck. (Also, she thoughtfully remembered to go and thank them for granting it at the end of the day.) Three very nice Frenchmen unloaded the large container into a smaller shuttle truck, which they then navigated down our narrow street and through our iron gates!

After placing furniture and boxes in the parlor, "Dear Lesley" (right) and the French moving crew take a break in the kitchen.

Once a load was transported to the house, Dad and I stationed ourselves outside near the truck and the front door — each with a copy of the inventory list — to check off the 176 numbered packages as they were removed. After three trips in the shuttle, all was unloaded and inside the farmhouse.

With Lesley's help, we utilized the parlor for most of the unwrapping, and then directed the movers to the proper rooms. They did all the unpacking, set up the beds and unrolled carpets so the house at rue du Clos de Paris can begin to look and feel like home. There's lots to put away, curtains to hang, and painting to be finished (Andre worked away, unfazed by the movers), so it was a good plan to have the French House available to us for two more weeks.

Me, checking off items in the shuttle truck, which made three trips to deliver our furnishings from the large moving van because it couldn't fit on the narrow rue.

We're exhausted, but extremely happy and grateful. This morning when we heard that cuckoo bird calling, we just looked at each other and grinned.

Love, Mom

A stone wall, floor mats, and a little red car

Dear Family,

As you round the corner coming down the street from the center of our small village, the stone end wall of the *petite maison* is the first glimpse you get of our house. Over the years, the wall has been patched (at times, unsuccessfully) with a variety of mortar colors. Simon has set out to render the stones with new mortar. He explained to me that he makes his mortar by mixing lime and sand — without cement — so the wall can breathe and moisture can escape. And, just like Cyril, the hue of the sand that Simon uses will determine the color of the mortar.

Yesterday, as I unpacked items to set in their new environs, I could hear Simon outside tap, tap, tapping to remove the old, multi-colored mortar between each stone. Going outside to check on his progress, I found him covered from head to toe in fine mortar dust. At the end of the day, he'd chipped away all of the old material by hand, and I could see how much better the wall already appears. He'll be back next week to re-mortar and brush each stone, which he promises will make this old wall the finest and strongest in all of Fresnay.

In some houses in France, floor tiles are set at the entryways around rectangular holes bordered in metal. In our house, there are four such spaces, all with different dimensions. The idea is that mats are placed down inside them, so they will stay in place without slipping. It's a *bonne idée*, except when you have no idea how to find the mats in order to purchase them. As there are literal "holes" in the floor, this is a real problem.

During renovations, Dad and I were repeatedly informed that we could easily locate a natural fiber material in rolls and have it cut to fit our specifications. After several unsuccessful attempts to locate them at stores that we'd been told would surely have them, voilà, we found them today. They are now snug in the trunk of our rental car, ready to fill the voids in the floors at the French Farmhouse tomorrow.

But the big success of the day was the purchase of our new French car. Dad had done some research and settled on a Clio Series 4 — in red, which he'd located in Brest, a town some hours away in Brittany. He'd also located a dealership in Le Mans, so in between floor mat shopping, we met with a delightful sales agent,

Charlotte, who blessedly spoke English. She arranged to have the car delivered to her dealership within two weeks. I promised to arrange for the bank wire and insurance, and we were all delighted to seal the deal. Steve and I celebrated with a splendid dinner at Chez Mariette, on our way back to the French House.

Hope you are all doing well! We love and miss you!

Mom

Before and after views of a side wall of the new family room, which was formerly the doctor's office and waiting room.

The long and winding road

We're still in the midst of unpacking and setting up the French Farmhouse for our move. Here's what's happening.

Dear Grown Kids, Granddaughter, and Daughter-in-law-to-be,

This chandelier is well traveled. We plucked it from a group being sold at a deep discount at a nearby Orlando Country Club, during the Club's renovations. My friend, Denise, accompanied me for the purchase. She wheedled the manager into lifting each heavy light fixture up off the floor, where they'd been clustered, so that we could view their bottoms and ensure we got one in the very best shape. Then she offered to sit with it in the open car trunk for the ride back through our neighborhood. (Now that's a great friend!) I demurred, and we fashioned another way to secure it for the ride home.

Dad and I then shipped the fixture to California, as a present to you, Leigh Anne. You soon left for your sojourn in India, so Google paid for the chandelier to sit for several years in a California storage unit. Last year, when you moved, the light fixture, along with other furnishings inherited from Mimi, found their way back to Orlando, to sit in yet another storage unit in Florida — this time paid for by us. In May, this same chandelier arrived in France by boat, along with our other household belongings. Today, we think it has finally found a permanent home — although the steeply discounted price is now not so steep!

We knew the traveling light fixture required retrofitting for French electrical current, so we rode with Petit Thierry to the electrical supply place — turning *à gauche* and *à droite* as he directed us between his horrid bouts of smoker's cough. Relieved to discover that it would be less than thirty euros to purchase the necessary supplies, we made our way home with our latest electrician hacking in the backseat and refusing a cough drop. Arriving at the French Farmhouse, we were greeted by another of Andre's friends, Grand Thierry, who is helping to sand the upstairs' bedroom doors, which had thankfully been brought outside for that purpose. Once parked, our noisy but extremely affable passenger emerged from the backseat — and immediately lit another cigarette.

Love, Mom/Kiki

*Simon, Andre, Petit Thierry, and Steve conferring on the best
way to hang the chandelier... mission almost accomplished!*

Romain, and Renault

Dear Family,

I wouldn't recommend scheduling your first hair salon appointment, and finishing up the renovation of a centuries-old farmhouse in France during the same week. I'm not sure which caused me more trepidation, but I guess it would be the hair. I had visions of coordinating my summer outfits with the bag I'd be wearing over my head. However, Romain (pronounced like the lettuce) recommended by Valerie, who has provided my manicures for the past several years in France, proved to be a superb hairdresser. After conveying French phrases for, "I don't want eggplant colored roots" to "My bangs shrink when they dry," I think Romain got the color and cut just right. His coiffure services came complete with a thorough washing and drying (really) of my ears, plus a sensual head massage!

If that wasn't enough excitement, it was time to collect our new car at the Renault dealership. Dad and I arrived after lunch, because in France even car salesmen break for a two-hour *déjeuner*. At the showroom, we were led to a car blanketed in a Renault car cover. With much fanfare, a salesman — Charlotte was

on *vacances* — whipped off the cloth to display our spanking new Clio. He then opened the driver's door and pulled out a bottle of champagne as a gift from the dealership — which I'm sipping as I write. (Shouldn't everyone receive a bottle of champagne when they buy a new car?)

During this darling ceremony, your Dad was absolutely beside himself with joy. And I was thinking... what in the world have we done? Underneath the showroom lights, the car looked more flambé than red. I worried that while in France we'd be driving a vehicle for the next ten years more suitable for Halloween. Fortunately, once outside the car is a definite *rouge*, and it couldn't be more perfect for us. We returned to the car rental agency one last time, thanked our trusty Europcar agent, Celine, and promised to send her all our visiting friends. We received comments such as "Wow" and *"Très belles"* from the workmen when we arrived at the French Farmhouse. I told them all that we'd picked a *tranquille* color — exactly like Monsieur Miller's personality!

Love, Mom

Steve, in the driveway at Clos de Paris with our new Clio,
which came with a full gas tank and a bottle of champagne!

Moving in, friends, and soirées

Dear Family,

How to describe the last few days? As we packed to leave the French House, Dad remarked that we'd normally be preparing to return to the U.S. about this time, as we'd been in France exactly one month — the former length of our sojourns here. One of the reasons we purchased the French Farmhouse was to have the ability to come and go as it suited us. So, as Andre completed his painting downstairs, our electrician hung the light fixtures in the master bathroom, and Lesley and Sherry made another run at removing the plaster dust, Dad and I moved a few hundred meters down the street — rather than back across the ocean.

It's difficult to recount our emotions. We first saw the "new" 18th century house nearly two years ago, and we immediately began to dream of how we could transform it into our home in France. After extensive investigating, plotting, planning, and implementing, we were actually going to be living in the house. I wish I could tell you that we celebrated triumphantly, but we were just plain exhausted. We did sleep well, even without the bedroom rug, bathroom doorknobs, or much warmth except from our space heater.

As the draperies are not yet hung, our shutters will have to suffice — which helped when Andre arrived early the next morning to continue his work upstairs. Leaving the house in his good hands, we met Annie and Tim in Alençon on Saturday for a flower and plant fair. Leaving with cars stuffed with beautiful flowers for our new pots, we continued on to their lovely home near Sees for coffee and dessert, and to check out their new gravel. We left with a baggie of sample stones, to see if we should purchase the same combination of colored pebbles for our terrace. (We should!)

I've often told you that the bonus to our life in France, along with the great scenery, wine, and food are the people. (I won't call them characters!) I have mentioned our neighbor, Guy, before. Well, I have decided that he's Dad's twin — on steroids. Guy and Regine live and work in Paris, and they have a second home on our street in Fresnay. In addition, they have a small farm just outside our village, where Guy keeps bees. After he'd popped out of his doorway earlier in our stay, to present us with a present of his special production of honey, he then invited us to visit his beehives on a Sunday afternoon. Even though there was (is) still much to do at our French Farmhouse, we accepted.

As I said, Dad and Guy are kindred spirits, each with abundant energy and numerous hobbies. Needless to say, Regine and I can relate. However, Guy takes it up a notch or two. He's currently attempting to attract a new queen to one of his beehives. But along with the bee enterprise and his job as a sales consultant for a San Francisco marketing firm, he's a blacksmith, singer, and musician — and he's learned how to repair rush seats in chairs (growing the reeds first) merely because he was interested in learning the process! After some wine and lively conversation at their farm, we waved *à bientôt* as they left for Paris and we returned to Fresnay.

During the past few days, Dad and I have worked on the house — room by room — hanging pictures and placing rugs. One night, to make our task more enjoyable, we popped open and drank champagne. I was relieved the next morning to discover that all had been hung properly!

Steve, making his task easier with a little bubbly on the side.

Our crew continues to mortar stone walls outside, and to paint, tile, and hang light fixtures inside. (We're now five border tiles short of finishing our shower. It's definitely the bathroom project which refuses to end!) On Monday, we potted flowers and placed outdoor furniture on the terrace just in time for an impromptu soirée. Two neighbors, who were returning to England, wanted to see the house before they left. They brought several friends along, and with the weather cooperating, we played host on the terrace for the first time. It was splendid!

Love, Mom

The terrace — made ready for an upcoming fête!

The table is laid in the parlor with party food.

A soirée to thank all of our hard workers and their families for their labors, which made the house at Clos de Paris into our new French home.

Bridge, and a birthday

I hope you're all having a good week, and that Campbell is enjoying her summertime break from school. Here's what's happening on our side of the planet.

Dear Family,

One of the visitors who came to our first soirée is a lady in her eighties. Micheline was born in Paris, but worked for many years as a department store buyer for ladies' lingerie in Canada. She retired to Fresnay, and she invited me to join her bridge group here. This should prove a challenge in many respects, one of which is that they begin play at 8:30 p.m. and continue until 11:30 p.m. — well past my bedtime! Another one, of course, is the language — darned if they don't all speak only in French!

It seems that Madame (the former mistress of our house, who now lives in Les Mans) had been a member of this bridge group, and they needed a replacement. Micheline wanted me to join them this coming Monday night. I begged off for more time to rest up prior to such an auspicious undertaking! She replied that she'd see me at the bridge table in two weeks!

After a meltdown today in yet another big-box store, I marched outside while tossing a quip over my shoulder to Dad, informing him that I hadn't moved to France so I could spend all of my time in these modern monstrosities. We seem to be almost finished with searching up and down aisles for items we need, so we should soon be able to spend our time more enjoyably — at least that's what Dad promised today.

Anyway, I'll end our news on a better note by telling you that yesterday was John's birthday. After all the workmen assisted in putting the radiators back in place against the freshly painted walls, we had cake with candles to celebrate. Lesley and Sherry, who'd been cleaning old paint and glue from the clay tiles on the floor of the master bedroom, joined the party. When you see my pictures, you'll see the little guy, Thierry, our consumptive electrician. He supplied us with the matches for the birthday candles!

Love, Mom

A bounty of cherries from the property, along with fresh items from the market.

Simon, Andre, Thierry, John, Lesley, and Sherry celebrating John's birthday in the new kitchen.

Teamwork, and a (sort of) finale

Dear Family,

Dad made a comment the other day that reminded me of an incident that occurred on a trip to Europe with Leigh Anne and my parents in the 80s. Utilizing my travel agent's discount, I'd booked us into a five star hotel in Switzerland. Leigh Anne and I strolled around the spacious accommodations, admiring the lovely views of Lake Lucerne and the beautiful marbled bathroom.

Videotape players were still nouveau then, and one had been installed in our hotel room. In that day and time, you would select a movie from a menu provided by the hotel, and then retrieve it from the staff in the lobby. We decided upon a Steve Martin comedy suitable for a twelve-year-old, and we made our request downstairs. A formally attired concierge handed our selection to us, while solemnly saying in thickly accented English, "Eerr izz zee film, Madame, 'Zee Man Wizz Two Brrainzz.'"

Now back to Dad's remark. He stated that it's taken both our brains to plan and implement this great adventure. He solved tricky construction issues and supplied lots of brawn, while I handled the banking, insurance, and contractor payments. Both of us oversaw the renovation and managed all the worker bees. It's taken beaucoup teamwork, and taxed both of us to the max.

While we still have plenty to keep us occupied all summer (i.e. the orange runner that is glued rather than tacked onto three sets of stairs on the staircase), including a desire to obtain a greater comfort level with the language, we're situated enough to feel at home here. We realize that we're blessed to live in two such diverse locations, living lives we look forward to in each place.

I thank you for sharing this two-year project along the way — from purchase, to renovation and relocation, with a peek at village life in between. I have appreciated your loving and supportive replies in return. Dad and I joyfully anticipate your frequent visits with us at rue du Clos de Paris in La Petite Cité de Caractère, Fresnay-sur-Sarthe.

À bientôt and lots of love, Mom

C'est fini!

Epilogue

The neighborhood rooster,
paying a visit to our terrace.

As you can imagine, work on a centuries-old French Farmhouse is never actually *fini*. During the months after our move, we continued our labors on the house. Tongue and groove shutters were constructed by Steve and Simon out of a chestnut tree — which had been reserved, cut, cured in a kiln, and delivered in planks still bearing bark — to be placed on the street side of the Grand Maison. This was not easily accomplished on a three-story building with a straight drop onto the steeply sloped *rue* below.

For the installation, our attorney friend, Tom, a.k.a. "Rope Man," stood dangling the lassoed eight-foot shutters out of the third-story windows, while Simon hung from a tow rope out of the second floor openings in order to screw in the fittings. Balancing on a tall ladder outside, Steve rounded out this daring installation crew. I tried not to watch, but all was accomplished without mishap, and with the blessing of the mayor and the Sarthe Historical and Architectural Committee.

On another beautiful fall day, six able-bodied helpers turned up with shovels and wheelbarrows to spread newly delivered gravel, selected from Tim and Annie's sample. It had been deposited in the street by an enormous dump truck, which had backed down the narrow *rue*. The golden mixture brought new life to the terrace, enhancing the pots of flowering plants placed prominently in strategic locations.

In our absence the following winter, Simon and Andre finished out the second floor bathrooms, laundry room, and backstairs. The interior of the house was finally ready for visitors, and we certainly had them throughout our second summer at the French Farmhouse! Family and friends christened the upstairs *chambres*, and the new master suite and communal rooms downstairs functioned well. Fine meals, cooked up with fresh ingredients scoured from local markets were produced in the new cuisine, and happily consumed on the terrace overlooking the River Sarthe — along with copious amounts of wine.

But the transformation was not yet complete. That same summer, Simon, John, and Les also removed tons of crumbling, old stucco from the exterior, and re-rendered all of the outside walls. Along with the freshly painted shutters completed by Andre and Moyen Thierry, the exterior of the house once again appears cheerful and inviting. Meanwhile, Monsieur Roulin continues to nurture the gardens and trees, and Lesley and Sherry keep the interior polished and shining. With all of these efforts, the home and grounds have slowly but surely reclaimed their former glory.

A recent ladybug invasion — symbols of good luck — provided us with a quirky sign of our good fortune in acquiring the French Farmhouse. Now, whenever Steve and I rhetorically ask each other if it was the right decision to purchase the property at Clos de Paris, we just look at each other and smile. Many, many thanks to all who made this all possible, and to our family and friends who have supported us all along the way!

À bientôt, Kyle and Steve

120

89091014R00075

Made in the USA
Columbia, SC
08 February 2018